W9-BHW-329

IOWA

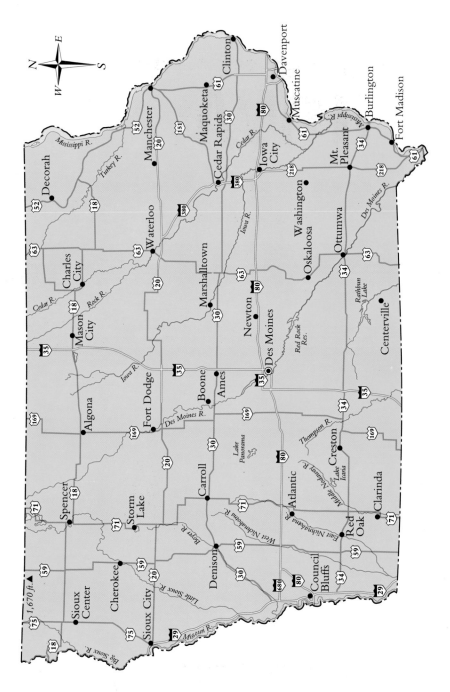

IOWA BY ROAD

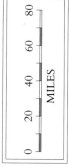

MILES

0   20   40   60   80

CELEBRATE THE STATES
IOWA

Polly Morrice

BENCHMARK BOOKS

MARSHALL CAVENDISH
NEW YORK

Benchmark Books
Marshall Cavendish Corporation
99 White Plains Road
Tarrytown, New York 10591-9001

Library of Congress Cataloging-in-Publication Data
Morrice, Polly Alison.
Iowa / Polly Morrice.
p.   cm. — (Celebrate the states)
Includes index.
Summary: Discusses the geographic features, history, government, people,
and attractions of the Midwestern state known for its rich farmland.
ISBN 0-7614-0421-X (lib. bdg.)
1. Iowa—Juvenile literature. [1. Iowa.] I. Title. II. Series.
F621.3.M67   1998   977.7—dc21   97-5177   CIP   AC

Maps and graphics supplied by Oxford Cartographers, Oxford, England

Photo Research by Matthew J. and Ellen B. Dudley

Cover Photo: *The Image Bank*, Alvis Upitis

The photographs in this book are used by permission and through the courtesy of: *Carl Kurtz*: 6- 7, 24, 12 (right), 129. *Photo Researchers, Inc.*: Andy Levin, 10-11; John Eastcott/Yva Momatiuk, 18; Norris Taylor, 50-51; Michael P. Gadomski, 61; Jeff Greenberg dMRp, 74; Ken M. Highfill, 121 (left). *Ty Smedes*: 15, 16, 19, 22, 26, 59, 68-69, 76, 84, 88-89, 102-103, 111, 116, 117, 124, 125, 127. *Bill Field*: 20, 57, 60, 119. *Cedar Rapids Museum of Art*: 28-29. *National Museum of American Art, Washington D.C./Art Resource NY*: 32. *The Mississippi River Museum, Dubuque, Iowa, Mural by James E. McBurney*: 33. *Corbis-Bettman*: 35, 46, 91 (bottom), 98 (top), 100, 130, 131 (top), 132 (right and left), 133. *State Historical Society of Iowa, Iowa City*: 37, 39, 43, 45. *University Art Collection, Iowa State University, Ames Iowa, Mural by Grant Wood*: 38. *State historical Society of Iowa, Des Moines*: 48. ©1996 *The Des Moines Register & Tribune Company/Photo by Bill Neibergall. Reprinted with permission*: 49. *A/P Wide World Photos*: 55. *Kay Shaw*: 64, 72, 136. *The Image Bank*: Lou Jones, 65; Kaz Mori, back cover. *Clinton Herald*: Jerry Dahl, 78. *Steve Ohrn*: 79, 80. *The Des Moines Register RAGBRAI*: 83. *Penfeild Press/Liffering-Zug*: 87. *UPI/Corbis-Bettman*: 91 (top), 93, 94, 131 (center), 131 (bottom), 134, 135 (left). *Frank Driggs/Corbis-Bettman*: 96. *Grant Wood, American, 1891-1942, American Gothic, oil on beaver board, 1930, 74.3 x 62.4cm., Friends of the American Art Collection, All rights reserved by The Art Institute of Chicago and VAGA, New York, NY 1930. 934. photograph ©1997, The Art Institute of Chicago, all rights reserved*: 98. (bottom). *National Parks Service*: 105. *Willowbrook Photography*: 106. *Iowa Tourism*: 108, 115. *Czech and Slovak Museum and Library*: 112. *Office of the Governor of the State of Iowa*: 120. *Springer/Corbis-Bettman*: 135 (top).

Printed in Italy

3   5   6   4   2

CONTENTS

IOWA IS....

Iowa is beautiful land . . .

"Taking this Territory, all in all, for convenience of navigation, water, fuel and timber; for richness of soil; for beauty of appearance, and for pleasantness of climate, it surpasses any portion of the United States with which I am acquainted."

—Lieutenant Albert M. Lea, explorer

. . . rich in natural grandeur.

"On the 23rd we had the quietest and heaviest fall of snow I ever witnessed even in this State of Wonders." —early settler Bella Williams

"Boy, the wind does blow sometimes! This flat, open ground runs clear to Winnipeg, and God only knows where it ends after that."

—Bob White, farmer from Peterson

Many people reaped bounty from the land . . .

"The fertility of the soil of Iowa is unsurpassed—not merely by that of her kindred States—not merely in our Union—but throughout the world!" —Iowa promoter Nathan H. Parker, 1856

. . . while others revered it.

"My reason teaches me that land cannot be sold. The great Spirit gave it to his children to live upon, and cultivate, as far as it is necessary for their subsistence; and so long as they occupy and cultivate it, they have the right to the soil. . . . Nothing can be sold but such things as can be carried away." —Sauk chief Black Hawk

Iowans are self-sufficient . . .

"What these Iowans don't already have, they figure they don't need." —character in Meredith Willson's *The Music Man*

. . . modest about their achievements . . .

"Iowa has never had the rampant boosterism of Kansas and Missouri. It has always been far too deprecating and self-doubting for that." —novelist Ruth Suckow

. . . and proud of their state's possibilities.

"Ours is a state of good people, closely tied to the rhythms of nature with a stability and resilience that was, and still is uncommon. We must seize this day, and fashion a future string of endless success stories: of families coming back home for good paying jobs; of communities with new leaders and new life; of a state known for steady growth." —Iowa governor Terry Branstad

---

Iowa means different things to different people. Some see its rolling acres of corn and peaceful towns as symbols of a way of life that has vanished elsewhere. Others view its Midwestern character and small towns as marks of an ordinary sort of place. The truth is, Iowa overflows with riches: beautiful scenery, friendly people, festive events. Here is a state where the endless horizon casts a spell. Here is the story of Iowa.

1 THE MIDDLE BORDER

Iowa is world famous for its rich farmland. "Climb onto a roof-top almost anywhere in the state," says writer Bill Bryson, a native Iowan, "and you are confronted with a . . . sweep of corn as far as the eye can see."

Bryson's claim is an exaggeration, but it reflects an astonishing fact: nearly 90 percent of Iowa's total land is devoted to agriculture. The state owes its deep, black topsoil to geology—and to the tall prairie grasses that once seemed as limitless as today's cornfields.

INLAND SEAS AND GLACIERS

Millions of years ago, Iowa alternated between being covered with warm, shallow seas and being left high and dry, exposed to weathering and erosion. Each time the water ebbed, it deposited sediment—sand and dirt—that gradually hardened into rock. Repeated over and over, this process eventually created Iowa's bedrock: layers of sandstone, limestone, dolomite, and shale.

About two million years ago, great sheets of ice called glaciers began to move across the central plains of the present United States. The glaciers smoothed the land. They scooped out river valleys, scattered boulders, and, most important for Iowa's future, deposited the soil, stone, and sand that became the basis for

LAND AND WATER

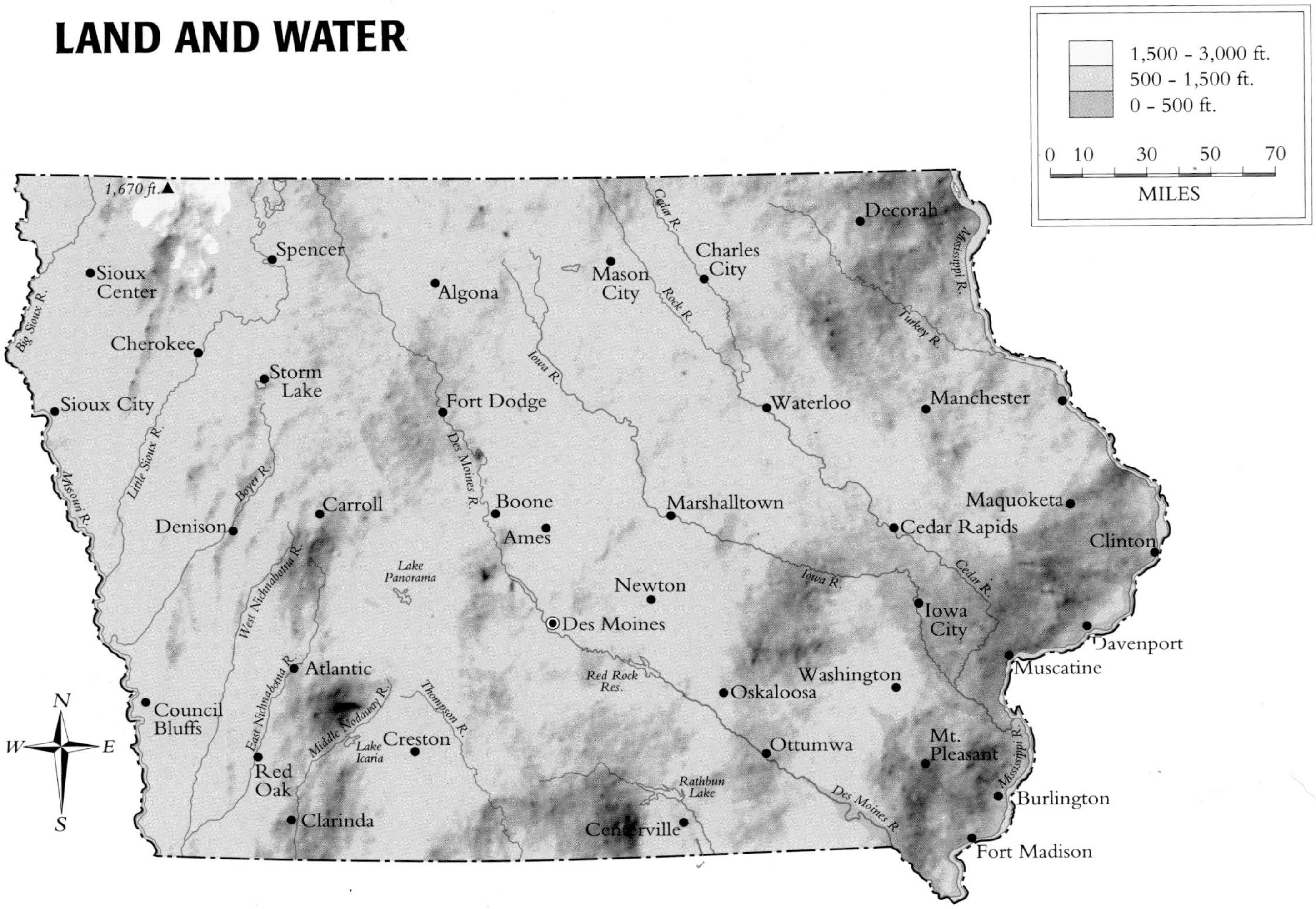

Sioux Center
Cherokee
Sioux City
Spencer
Storm Lake
Algona
Carroll
Denison
Council Bluffs
Atlantic
Red Oak
Creston
Clarinda
Fort Dodge
Boone
Ames
Des Moines
Newton
Centerville
Mason City
Charles City
Marshalltown
Decorah
Waterloo
Manchester
Cedar Rapids
Maquoketa
Clinton
Iowa City
Washington
Oskaloosa
Ottumwa
Mt. Pleasant
Davenport
Muscatine
Burlington
Fort Madison

Big Sioux R.
Little Sioux R.
Missouri R.
Boyer R.
Des Moines R.
West Nishnabotna R.
East Nishnabotna R.
Middle Nishnabotna R.
Thompson R.
Lake Icaria
Lake Panorama
Red Rock Res.
Iowa R.
Cedar R.
Rock R.
Turkey R.
Mississippi R.
Cedar R.
Iowa R.
Des Moines R.
Rathbun Lake

1,670 ft.

1,500 – 3,000 ft.
500 – 1,500 ft.
0 – 500 ft.

MILES
0 10   30   50   70

N
E
S
W

fertile topsoil. When the last glaciers receded, about ten thousand years ago, Iowa's terrain looked much as it does today.

Some people think that all of Iowa is as flat as a tabletop. Iowans know that most of the land in their state rolls gently. From the air, the neat square fields of corn, soybean, and hay suggest a manicured garden, dotted with red barns and white farmhouses. "It's an incredibly beautiful place," says a woman from Des Moines. "I feel lucky to have grown up there."

THE HEART OF THE COUNTRY

Hamlin Garland, one of Iowa's first successful writers, called his state "the Middle Border." The description is apt, since Iowa lies squarely in the middle of the north-central United States. Minnesota forms its northern border, Wisconsin and Illinois are located to the east, Missouri to the south, and South Dakota and Nebraska to the west.

Iowa poet Paul Engle once observed that the state has "the stylized outline of a hog, with the snout pushing east between Dubuque and Davenport." Other Iowans argue that, because of the small "panhandle" at its southeastern boundary, Iowa is shaped more like a miniature United States. Iowa's highest point, 1,670 feet, is on a family farm in the extreme northwest of the state; Iowa's lowest point of 480 feet is in the southeastern tip, along the Mississippi River.

A look at Iowa's regions reveals just how powerful the glaciers were. The northeastern section of the state experienced little glacial activity and is now known as "Little Switzerland." Rocky bluffs

Here is a view of the Mississippi River from Pikes Peak State Park in northeastern Iowa's "Little Switzerland" region.

and cliffs rise abruptly from the banks of the Mississippi River, reaching heights of four hundred feet. Valleys are steep, and trees are abundant.

North-central Iowa, by contrast, is considerably flatter. There, massive ice sheets carved out marshes, small lakes, and the depressions the early pioneers called "kettleholes." When settlers drained the boggy land, they found it contained some of the world's richest soil.

Most of the rest of the state is covered with gently rolling hills. The exception, which attracts tourists and geologists alike, are the Loess Hills in Iowa's extreme northwest, bordering the Missouri River. These hills resemble giant snow drifts. They were created from heaps of loess, or silt, that were deposited along the Missouri

Erosion etched these ridges—or "cat steps"—into the Loess Hills of western Iowa. Poet and essayist Michael Carey describes the hills as "green, mute, unfathomable, as if fallen from another world."

River by the glaciers, and then blown beyond the riverbank into hills. These wind-made dunes are found only in Iowa and some parts of China. The region's early Native Americans considered them sacred.

WATERWAYS

Iowa is the only state bordered by two navigable rivers. The mighty Mississippi flows the full length of its eastern boundary. On the west, the Big Sioux joins with the Missouri River at Sioux City; the Missouri then runs along the remainder of Iowa's border.

A low ridge curving from Dickinson County in northwest Iowa to Davis County in the state's southeast quadrant serves as the state's divide. Rivers located to its west, including the Big and Little Sioux and the Floyd, flow into the Missouri. Rivers east of the ridge, such as the Des Moines, central Iowa's largest river, flow into the Mississippi. Each year, millions of tons of cargo are shipped along the state's waterways.

Iowa can boast no large natural lakes, but many of its small ones are beautiful. In the northwest, the glaciers scooped out Iowa's "Great Lakes": Spirit Lake, Storm Lake, Clear Lake, and West and East Okoboji Lakes.

Scattered elsewhere are artificial lakes created by damming rivers. These reservoirs draw hordes of weekend fishers, swimmers, and picnickers. They include Coralville Lake, on the Iowa River; Lake Red Rock and Saylorville Lake, on the Des Moines River; and—largest of all—Rathbun Lake, on the Chariton River in extreme south-central Iowa.

THE GREAT FLOOD

During the summer of 1993, torrents of rain fell on the Midwest. In Iowa, so many rivers overran their banks that President Bill Clinton declared the entire state a disaster area.

Des Moines was particularly hard hit. The Raccoon River swept over the city, disabling the waterworks plant and leaving residents without running water for two weeks. They fought back by piling up 1.5 million sandbags and helping each other clean up flooded houses. Despite the hardships, many people felt the disaster had bolstered the city's spirit.

"Awful as it's been," said one woman, "it's also been oddly wonderful. It's made the city into one big family."

Iowa's waterways attract fishers of all ages.

"THE MOST EXCITING WEATHER"

The first white settlers in Iowa were lured by promises of a moderate, healthful climate. Iowa historian Glenda Riley jokes that "maybe there was some logic . . . which assumed that if Iowa was good for corn, it was good for people."

In fact, like all of the upper Midwest, Iowa has a climate of extremes. Its central location makes it a crossroads for air masses and fronts moving in from all directions. The resulting weather can be very dramatic. Sometimes the temperature drops fifty degrees in a single day.

The lowest temperature ever recorded in the state was -47 degrees, at Washta, in northwest Iowa, on January 12, 1912.

Growing up in Iowa means going to school in wintry weather.

January 1997 was nearly as severe. Even old-timers agreed that a windchill factor approaching 70 degrees below zero was some of the coldest weather *they* had ever experienced.

Iowa's harsh arctic winds, accompanied by heavy snowfall, produce the terrific storms called blizzards (the term was coined by a nineteenth-century Iowa journalist). Farmers have planted stands of trees that help break the force of the wind and prevent massive snowdrifts. Still, some blizzards are devastating. In April 1973, a blizzard caused fourteen deaths and $19 million in livestock losses.

During the spring and summer, Iowans witness awesome

thunderstorms. From May through August, the number of days lightning branches across darkened skies averages fifty. The same conditions that cause thunderstorms—warm updrafts of wind colliding with cold downdrafts—sometimes spawn tornadoes. These powerful "twisters" occur when winds blowing in opposite directions around an updraft begin to whirl violently; sometimes tearing roofs off houses and reducing groves of trees to timber. One Iowan recalls that after a tornado hit his grandfather's farm near Eagle Grove, the family found a straw driven into the plank of a barn.

Gail Schorre, an architect who grew up in Webster City, says, "I remember going out and seeing the clouds swirling into spiral shapes. It was the most exciting weather."

During an average season, Iowans report about thirty tornadoes and more than a hundred funnel clouds. Iowa suffers more tornadoes for its area than any other state.

A LONG GROWING SEASON

Although Iowa's climate can be hard on people, it is nearly perfect for agriculture. Rainy springs, combined with long, hot growing seasons (150 days, on average), produce bountiful crops. Iowa's highest known temperature was 118 degrees, measured at Keokuk, in the state's southern tip, on July 20, 1934. More usually, mid-summer temperatures hover in the mid- to high eighties. The hot days and nights contribute to successful corn crops. Even the blanket of snow that covers Iowa from December until March is useful, because it helps store moisture in the earth for spring planting. And it contributes to the twenty-six to thirty-six inches of precipitation that fall on the state.

Most Iowans take pride in their state's changeable weather and in their ability to adapt to it. "Some years, on my birthday, there would be flowers blooming," recalls Gail Schorre, who was born on March 28. "In other years we'd have a snow day and miss school."

FOREST AND PRAIRIE

Before the settlers came, woodlands covered 20 percent of Iowa, mainly along the Mississippi River and around streams. So many

With its red barn, white house, and tall silos, this farm in Decorah is typical of many Iowa farms.

trees were cut down to build cabins and for other uses that now only 4 percent of Iowa is forested.

Yet white oak and hickory forests still grow on the state's slopes and hilltops. In river floodplains, cottonwoods thrive. Each autumn their leaves turn a multitude of colors: golds, reds, and browns.

Iowa has preserved even less of its greatest natural treasure: the prairies. In the early nineteenth century, nearly 80 percent of the state was covered with tallgrass prairies. Today, it is almost impossible to imagine the Iowa landscape that was first seen by Native Americans and early settlers. In letters and journals, the awed pioneers described the prairies as "seas of grass." The grass was so high it hid the tops of their covered wagons. In spring and summer, brilliant wildflowers transformed the prairie into "one great flower garden," according to a delighted pioneer woman.

The prairie grasses, such as big bluestem and Indian grass, contributed to the sixteen- to twenty-four-inch layer of topsoil that so impressed the newcomers. Wayne Petersen, a conservationist with the Natural Resources Conservation Service in Johnson County, says that "Iowa owes its rich soil to prairie vegetation that contributes more organic matter each year to the soil than a forest." Unlike tree roots, which live for years, the roots of prairie grasses die annually and then decompose, enriching the soil.

By 1900, almost all of Iowa's great prairie had been plowed under. It was replaced by cultivated fields with ribbons of road running through them. Nowadays, only about three thousand acres of native prairie are left. Some remnants can be found in ditches or old cemeteries, but most remaining prairies are protected in state preserves such as Hayden Prairie, near Cresco in eastern Iowa.

Iowans have reconstructed parts of the vast sea of grass that once spread over the state.

Over the past thirty years, some Iowans have joined a movement to recreate this element of their state's natural heritage. They have started small prairies of their own. Paul Christiansen of Mount Vernon is a prairie enthusiast. "We're throwing away a lot of knowledge if we don't preserve prairie species and their interactions," he says. "It would be like burning a library or museum and losing the information there. Once it's gone, it's gone."

WILDLIFE

Farming and settlement also affected Iowa's animal populations. The state's prairies, woodlands, and wetlands once teemed with wildlife. Herds of bison, elk, and deer grazed in the fields; otters and beaver splashed in rivers and streams. Twice a year the skies turned black with migrating passenger pigeons.

The settlers hunted many of these animals to extinction. Other species vanished when their habitats disappeared. The plowing of the prairies threatened the survival of the prairie chicken. Similarly, when farmers drained swampy land, they destroyed nesting sites for wildfowl. One hundred years ago, Iowa's wetlands totaled six million acres. Today, only about forty thousand acres remain.

Fortunately, Iowa still provides nesting grounds for many birds, including quail, pheasants, and wild turkeys. Canada geese rest in Iowa fields during migration periods. Bird-watchers sometimes spot a great horned owl or a bald eagle.

Thirty years ago, the white-tailed deer, whose numbers had dropped sharply, became a protected animal in Iowa. The state's deer population now numbers three hundred thousand, but the

Prairie chickens were once abundant in Iowa, but hunting and farming reduced their numbers and destroyed their nesting places. Wildlife expert James Dinsmore writes that the state "no longer supports a population of the bird most symbolic of the prairie habitat."

increase has brought it into direct conflict with people. Each year, Iowa records eleven thousand accidents between deer and cars.

PRESERVING THE ENVIRONMENT

Iowa farmers are taking measures to preserve the state's natural resources. After the prairies were converted to farmland, Iowa's miraculous topsoil was threatened by erosion. In many places, the original sixteen- to twenty-four-inch layer has been reduced to eight inches.

Serious efforts at conserving Iowa's topsoil began in the 1930s. Today, the state employs experts to advise farmers on the best techniques for preventing erosion. Many farmers develop systems of their own, such as building terraces and plowing their hilly fields on a contour.

Iowans are also trying to restore their wetlands. The Iowa River Corridor Project, funded by the federal government, is seeking to re-create wetlands along nearly forty-three miles of the Iowa River. By returning acres of corn and hay to strips of wetland, the project will reduce flooding and improve the river's water quality.

With nearly three million people, Iowa will never return to its wilderness state. But modern Iowans are facing the challenge of conserving what is left of their natural heritage.

Clint Fraley, an outdoorsman and a member of the Clay County Conservation Board, says the best way to encourage conservation is to start with school kids. "I just want to get people excited," he says. "You can't force anybody to get interested in anything, but if you once get them into it, get them out on the prairie or into the woods, they might take off on their own and might get really excited."

2 BECOMING IOWA

July Clouds, *by Martin Cone*

The earliest Iowans were nomadic hunters. Twelve thousand years ago, they stalked mastodons, mammoths, and other prehistoric animals. When the climate grew warmer and these large species became extinct, the native peoples changed their way of life. They invented new weapons for hunting bison, deer, and elk. Eventually they settled in villages and began growing corn and squash.

TRADERS AND MOUND BUILDERS

By 500 B.C., at least five prehistoric cultures inhabited Iowa. Among these were the Woodland people, who had mastered pottery making. From villages on the Mississippi River, they traded their wares with tribes from as far away as the Rocky Mountains.

The Woodland people were mound builders. Each year families gathered to construct great earthworks—made of dirt and stones— which were used for burying their dead and for other religious purposes. While many of these low mounds were circular in shape with conical or flat tops, others took the forms of animals, such as birds and bears. Great care went into creating these works, which have survived many centuries.

Other mound-building cultures also thrived in Iowa before the Europeans came. The Glenwood people lived in large, sunken lodges in southwestern Iowa; the Mill Creek people settled along the Big and Little Sioux Rivers.

Around A.D. 1300, the climate shifted again, becoming warmer and drier. The change apparently weakened the Mill Creek and other cultures, and a rival group called the Oneota pushed them out of the state. The Oneota, who built villages throughout Iowa, were likely the ancestors of the Ioway, the tribe that white explorers encountered some three hundred years later.

BEAUTIFUL LANDS

In 1673, the French explorers Louis Jolliet and Father Jacques Marquette set out from northern Michigan to find the mouth of the Mississippi River. After crossing Wisconsin, they launched their canoes into the Mississippi at the present-day Iowa town of McGregor. Paddling downstream, they glimpsed Iowa's green, lush hills. "Beautiful lands," noted Marquette in his diary. On June 25, they went ashore on the western side of the river, becoming the first Europeans to set foot on Iowa soil.

Ten years later, the French explorer Robert Cavelier, Sieur de La Salle, claimed the entire Mississippi River valley for France. He christened the vast territory Louisiana, for King Louis XIV.

During the next hundred years, few Europeans ventured into the Iowa grasslands. Occasionally, French fur traders roved west of the Mississippi to trap beaver. In the mid-1700s, two new Indian groups moved in. Driven from their native Wisconsin, the Mesquakie (Fox) and Sauk settled along the Mississippi River bluffs, in what is today Illinois and eastern Iowa.

The Sauk and Mesquakie Indians, depicted in this 1837 painting by George Catlin, were relative newcomers to Iowa, arriving in the mid-eighteenth century.

Iowa's first permanent white resident, Julien Dubuque, arrived in 1788. He was an ambitious French Canadian who had received a large land grant in northeastern Iowa. A friend to the Indians, Dubuque married the daughter of the Mesquakie chief. He successfully mined lead on his lands, which extended for miles along the Mississippi River.

BECOMING UNITED STATES TERRITORY

In 1803, desperate for cash, the French emperor Napoléon sold all 828,000 square miles of Louisiana Territory to the United States. The price was $15 million—less than four cents an acre. Vast new lands, including the wilderness of Iowa, became part of the United States.

At first, Iowa was off-limits to white settlers. By order of the U.S. government, all land west of the Mississippi still belonged to the Indians. Easterners were starting to become interested, though. They had read the glowing reports of the new territory written by Meriwether Lewis and William Clark, whom President Thomas Jefferson had dispatched to explore the immense Louisiana

Julien Dubuque, Iowa's first permanent white settler, won the Indians' affection.

Purchase. In the spring of 1804, Lewis and Clark had paddled north along the Missouri River, passing the bluffs and grasslands of western Iowa. Another expedition that grazed Iowa's shores was led by Lieutenant Zebulon Pike. Setting out from St. Louis in 1805, Pike followed the Mississippi north, scouting likely sites for U.S. military forts.

In 1804, U.S. government agents tricked a small group of Sauk Indians into signing a harsh treaty. On behalf of their tribe, these Indians agreed to abandon their lands in Illinois and move across the river into Iowa. By 1830, they had reluctantly migrated to their new homes, where they planted crops and built villages.

But the Sauk did not possess these rich lands for long. Iowa's black soil proved too enticing to white settlers.

THE LAST BATTLE

In 1832, the aging Sauk leader Black Hawk led an uprising to regain the tribe's Illinois lands. The Black Hawk War, as it is called, was doomed from the start. For three months, the U.S. Army chased the old chief and his allies across northern Illinois and southern Wisconsin. Once Black Hawk was captured, the government punished the Sauk and Mesquakie peoples by seizing the narrow strip of land they had been awarded west of the Mississippi. It was opened for white settlement in 1833. Land-hungry farmers quickly rushed in.

Soon the government forced more treaties on the Indians. These agreements caused the Indians to give up even more acreage. In 1842, the government purchased the last remaining Iowa land held

Chief Black Hawk led the Sauk and Mesquakie in a losing fight to keep their lands along the Mississippi River. "I loved my towns, my cornfields, and the home of my people," he told the new white inhabitants of Iowa.

by the Sauk and Mesquakie. In 1846, the Winnebago Indians—which U.S. troops had moved into northern Iowa from Wisconsin—were also pushed out of the territory. Less than twenty years after Black Hawk mounted his desperate campaign, the Indian presence in Iowa was nearly ended. Today Iowa preserves the memory of the old chief in its nickname, the Hawkeye State.

FARMERS AND FAMILIES

Once Iowa was opened to white settlers, droves of newcomers arrived. They were drawn by exaggerated accounts of the area's riches. One newspaper promised that those who came "with strong minds and willing hands to work" would be "abundantly blessed and rewarded."

The first person to call the great prairies stretching between the Missouri and Mississippi River the "Iowa" territory was a young army lieutenant named Albert M. Lea. No one is sure what the names "Iowa" and "Ioway" originally meant. They may be misspellings of *ayuxwa*, an Indian word that means "drowsy ones." Other possible translations are "this is the place" and "beautiful land."

About a third of the new settlers migrated to Iowa from Illinois, Ohio, Indiana, Wisconsin, and Michigan. Others came from the south, traveling up the Mississippi on riverboats, while a third group crossed the Great Lakes and set out from Chicago in covered wagons.

CHILDREN ON THE TRAIL

Many of Iowa's early pioneers were children, from newborns to teenagers. Older kids had many chores to do, such as herding livestock. Younger ones were often threatened by illness and accidents. But kids are kids, and many of the youngest trail riders had fun on their trip west. They played tag among the covered wagons, gathered wildflowers, and made friends with children traveling in other caravans. One woman remembered her journey to Iowa this way: "Maybe it was hard for the grown folks, but for the children and young people it was just one long, perfect picnic."

Many of the settlers who came to Iowa in the 1840s traveled by steamer, proceeding up the Mississippi River to towns such as Dubuque—shown here as it looked in 1846.

Iowa became a magnet for immigrants from northern and western Europe. Some were fleeing famine at home. Others were escaping political turmoil. By 1870, nearly one-fifth of Iowa's residents had been born in foreign countries; they were Dutch, Irish, English, Scandinavian, and, in largest number, German.

Most newcomers became farmers. They laid claim to land in quarter or half sections (160 or 320 acres), paying $1.25 an acre for untilled soil. To prepare their land for planting, they hired a professional prairie breaker. He cut furrows through the dense, tangled roots of the prairie grasses with his "breaking plow," a huge contraption pulled by as many as sixteen oxen. In the eastern part of the state, the settlers built small log houses. In the west, where trees were scarcer, they used sod and prairie grass.

Although life on the prairie was often hard, nothing could stop the flow of immigrants. By 1850, Iowa had nearly two hundred thousand inhabitants.

THE ROAD TO STATEHOOD

Until 1838, Iowa belonged to the enormous Territory of Wisconsin. The population boom convinced the U.S. Congress to create a separate Territory of Iowa, and President Martin Van Buren

Before they could plant their first crops, the pioneers had to plow the tough prairie sod under. Most hired professional prairie breakers to do the job.

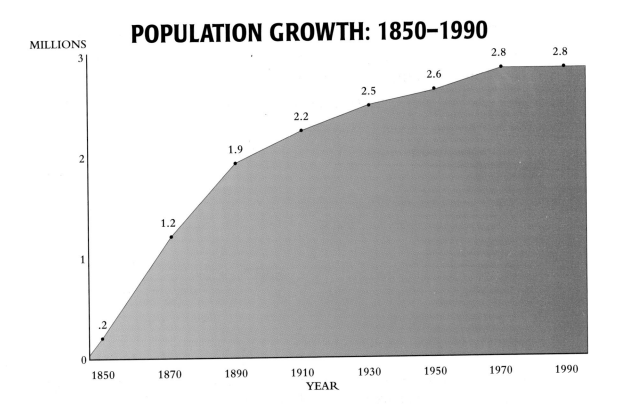

POPULATION GROWTH: 1850–1990

MILLIONS

appointed Robert Lucas as its first governor. Stern and decisive, Lucas set up county governments and appointed the first judges to the territory's supreme court. Lucas also built the territorial capitol, a handsome stone building that is now a landmark at the University of Iowa.

In 1844, the U.S. Congress voted to admit Iowa as a state. Iowans overwhelmingly rejected the offer, for good reason: the proposed state was too small! The boundaries Congress had drawn cut Iowa Territory nearly in half.

Legislators from Northern states had been responsible for divid-

LITTLE OLD SOD SHANTY ON THE PLAIN

"I've got a little bet with the government," said the homesteader. "They're betting me I can't live here for five years, and I'm betting them that I can." Under the terms of the Homestead Act of 1862, people could claim 160 acres of land for free, provided they worked and lived on the claim for five years. Most homesteaders stuck it out.

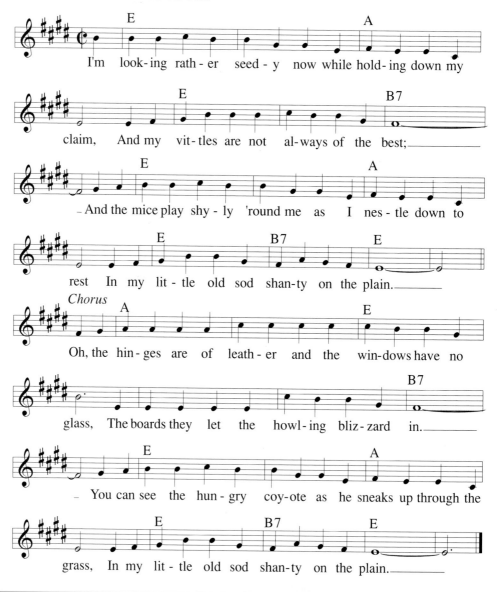

I'm look-ing rath-er seed-y now while hold-ing down my claim, And my vit-tles are not al-ways of the best; _ And the mice play shy-ly 'round me as I nes-tle down to rest In my lit-tle old sod shan-ty on the plain. _

Chorus
Oh, the hin-ges are of leath-er and the win-dows have no glass, The boards they let the howl-ing bliz-zard in. _ You can see the hun-gry coy-ote as he sneaks up through the grass, In my lit-tle old sod shan-ty on the plain. _

I rather like the novelty of living in this way,
Though my bill of fare isn't always of the Best,
But I'm happy as a clam on the land of Uncle Sam,
In my little old sod shanty in the West.   *Chorus*

But when I left my Eastern home, a bachelor so gay,
To try and win my way to wealth and fame,
I little thought I'd come down to burning twisted hay
In the little old sod shanty on my claim.   *Chorus*

My clothes are plastered o'er with dough, I'm looking like a fright,
And everything is scattered round the room;
But I wouldn't give the freedom that I have out in the West
For the table of the Eastern man's old home.   *Chorus*

Still, I wish that some kind-hearted girl would pity on me take,
And relieve me from the mess that I am in;
The angel, how I'd bless her if this her home she'd make
In the little old sod shanty on my claim.   *Chorus*

And if fate should bless us now and then with an heir
To cheer our hearts with honest pride of fame,
Oh, then we'd be contented for the toil that we had spent
In the little old sod shanty on our claim.   *Chorus*

When time enough had lapsed and all those little brats
To noble man and womanhood had grown,
It wouldn't seem half so lonely as round us we should look,
And we'd see the old sod shanty on our claim.   *Chorus*

Robert Lucas was the first governor of Iowa Territory. He had never seen the Iowa country until he arrived in Burlington, in August 1838, to take up his appointment.

ing up Iowa Territory. They hoped to bring two new states into the Union, instead of just one. Since Iowa prohibited slavery, the new states carved from it would be free states. Northerners thought this would ensure that the country's slave states did not outnumber the free ones.

Iowa finally became a state in 1846, after its western boundary was extended to the Missouri River. Iowa was admitted to the Union along with Florida, which allowed slavery. The arrangement satisfied some people, since it preserved the balance of power between the Northern and Southern states. But it did not solve the underlying tensions, which would lead to a bloody civil war.

IOWANS GO TO WAR

Iowa was the first free state west of the Mississippi River. It attracted many abolitionists, or people who worked to end slavery. Many participated in the Underground Railroad, helping slaves flee north toward Canada and freedom.

When the Civil War broke out in 1861, Iowa quickly rallied to the Union cause. During the four-year conflict, nearly 80,000 Iowans joined the army. Almost one in six died; another 8,500 were seriously wounded.

Back home, women supported their families by themselves and organized relief efforts. In Tama County, Marjorie Ann Rogers

Soldiers from the Mississippi River town of Bellevue set off to join the Union army in 1861.

taught herself to drive a team of horses and bring farm produce to market. Once, some men tried to help Rogers down from her wagon. She recalled that she "declined their kindness and said I would get down the same as a man if I could do a man's work."

The war brought other changes to Iowa, some in the political arena. In the mid-1850s, Iowans had begun supporting the new Republican Party because it was the antislavery party. After the war, Iowa became almost exclusively Republican in its politics. Its reputation as a one-party state lasted more than one hundred years. In 1885, an Iowa senator declared, "Iowa will go Democratic when Hell goes Methodist."

The war also affected Iowa's economy. The early settlers had been subsistence farmers who grew or made everything they needed. But during the war, many Iowans became large-scale commercial farmers. Despite poor transportation, they supplied huge amounts of food to the Union army.

Postwar farmers benefited from improved farm machinery. They also heeded advice from agricultural experts, who told them to raise corn rather than wheat. The stage was set for Iowa's emergence as one of the world's great food producers and exporters. All farmers needed was a better way to get their produce to market.

RAILROADS AND GRANGERS

Iowa's first railroad was completed in 1855. It ran between the Mississippi River towns of Muscatine and Davenport, a distance of thirty miles. By 1880, five major lines cut west across the state. Iowa farmers at last had access to national markets.

By 1890, Iowa led the nation in the production of corn and was second in the number of hogs raised. Railroads brought farmers prosperity, but sometimes they also threatened the farmers' livelihoods. The railroad companies had a monopoly on the prices they charged for shipping freight and carrying passengers. Often these prices were unreasonably steep. Since the railroad corporations controlled many politicians, there seemed little chance that railroad fares would ever be regulated by the government.

In the early 1870s, a major farm depression hit Iowa. The sharp loss of income brought farmers together to better their economic and political situation. The Grange, an organization formed to promote farmers' welfare, counted one hundred thousand Iowans among its members.

Since the mid-1800s, raising pigs—such as these Hampshire sows—has provided a major source of income for Iowa farmers.

The Grange set up its first Iowa branch in 1868. This Grange poster from 1876 shows how the farmer supports all ranks of society.

Iowa's Grangers demanded that the state set maximum prices the railroads could charge. In 1874, the state legislature passed the so-called Granger Law, which set up a state railroad commission. However, the commission was financed—and controlled—by the railroads themselves, which meant it had little power. Another fifteen years passed before real, effective railway regulations took effect, under the leadership of Governor William Larrabee.

Larrabee, a Republican, pursued policies that later became typical of the Progressive movement. Progressives sought to extend the government's power to regulate business. They also tried to increase popular participation in the political process. Their influence can still be seen in Iowa, whose voters sometimes surprise political observers.

"Despite [their] conservatism," says the *Des Moines Register*, "Iowans have a keen, perhaps mischievous, sense of balance. What, if not a balancing act, is sending liberal Tom Harkin to the U.S. Senate a third time to join three-term conservative Charles Grassley?"

THE TWENTIETH CENTURY

By 1900, most Iowans earned a comfortable living from agriculture. During the century's first two decades, corn prices rose, causing land values to soar—from $43 an acre in 1900 to $255 an acre twenty years later.

Then, prices for farm produce dropped abruptly. The 1920s brought hard times to farmers in Iowa and across the country. In October 1929, the stock market crashed, plunging the entire country into the Great Depression. For Iowa farmers, matters grew desperate. They sold their corn for ten cents a bushel—less than farmers had received in 1857!

The economic squeeze produced violence that is rare in Iowa's history. The most serious incident occurred during a farmers' strike that had been called to demand higher prices. In August 1932, farmers picketed the roads leading into Sioux City; they turned back

The Great Depression of the 1930s brought hard times to Iowa. In August 1932, desperate farmers set up a blockade outside Sioux City, trying to keep farm products from reaching the market and to demand higher prices for their own goods.

all trucks carrying farm produce to market. A group of pickets spotted a young man driving a milk truck. Although they ordered him not to cross the picket line, he kept going. One striker fired a gun, intending to frighten the driver away, but the bullet pierced the windshield and killed him. When the strikers emptied the cans loaded in the truck, they found, not milk, but bootleg whiskey. The driver had sped on for fear he would be caught breaking the national law against making liquor. "It was just a freak shot," said one observer, "but the kid was just as dead anyway."

Iowa is no longer a place where most people live on farms. In 1960, for the first time, more Iowans lived in urban areas than rural ones. By 1997, only about one in ten Iowans earned a living as a farmer. But the state's core industries of meatpacking, food processing, and farm-machinery manufacture remain tied to agriculture. And Iowa's spirit still draws on the state's agrarian roots.

In 1996, Iowans marked the 150th anniversary of becoming a state. In festivals throughout the year, they celebrated their history and looked forward to the future.

On December 28, 1996, residents threw themselves a big statehood party in the capital, Des Moines. At noon, Pat Powers of Webster City rang the state's Liberty Bell for nearly five minutes. Cars on nearby streets pulled over to listen.

Finally he was finished. "There!" he shouted. "Happy birthday, Iowa!"

In 1996, Iowa celebrated its 150th year as a state. At the official statehood party, Pat Powers rang the Iowa Liberty Bell.

3 CAUCUSES AND CORNFIELDS

The state capitol in Des Moines

"Iowans have a wonderful work ethic," says a man from Iowa City. Looking at the state's government and economy, it is easy to see how the residents have earned their reputation for hard work.

INSIDE GOVERNMENT

Since territorial days, Iowans have been active in civic affairs. They register to vote in high numbers: nearly 80 percent of those eligible do so. When Iowans go to the polls for statewide elections, they participate in a three-branch system of government put in place by the state constitution of 1857.

Like the federal model, Iowa's system ensures that power is distributed equally among the executive, judicial, and legislative arms of government. None of these branches can function without the consent of the people.

Legislative. The Iowa legislature is called the General Assembly. It consists of a senate and a house of representatives. The fifty senators serve four-year terms; the hundred representatives are elected every two years.

During legislative sessions, members consider hundreds of proposals for new laws and changes to existing laws. These bills can range from reinstating the death penalty to imposing taxes. They affect both day-to-day life and the state's future.

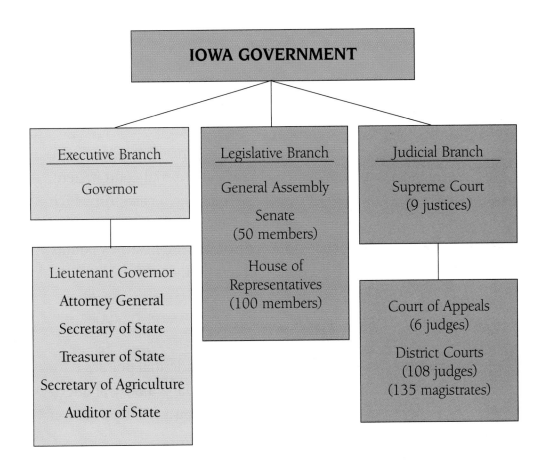

IOWA GOVERNMENT

Executive Branch

Governor

Lieutenant Governor

Attorney General

Secretary of State

Treasurer of State

Secretary of Agriculture

Auditor of State

Legislative Branch

General Assembly

Senate
(50 members)

House of
Representatives
(100 members)

Judicial Branch

Supreme Court
(9 justices)

Court of Appeals
(6 judges)

District Courts
(108 judges)
(135 magistrates)

Executive. Every four years Iowa voters elect a governor. As the state's chief officer, the governor proposes how funds should be spent, oversees the operation of twenty-two departments, and takes final action on all bills passed by the Iowa legislature. The governor can sign a bill to approve it, or veto a bill to reject it. The legislature can override this veto if two-thirds of both the senate and house vote to repass the bill. Voters also elect six other state administrators, including an attorney general and a secretary of agriculture.

Judicial. Iowa's judicial branch interprets the state's laws and settles conflicts involving them. The Iowa Supreme Court is the highest court in the state. Its nine members are appointed by the governor but, after serving a year, must receive voter approval to complete their full terms.

In 1976, Iowa established a state court of appeals to help resolve the backlog in its Supreme Court. There is also a trial court system, whose judges preside over criminal cases and civil cases (in which one person sues another). Cases that involve small amounts of money or minor crimes, called misdemeanors, are heard by county magistrates appointed by a special commission.

IOWA POLITICS AND THE NATION

Iowa may have a small population, but its presidential politics have a national impact. Every four years in late January, a bevy of television and newspaper reporters descends on Iowa. Caucus season has arrived!

Next come the presidential hopefuls, both Republicans and Democrats. They brave the state's wintry winds to address Rotary clubs and speak at rallies. Their goal is to win their party's Iowa caucuses, or at least make a strong showing.

Political caucuses are basically small meetings. On a Tuesday in February, groups of Republicans and Democrats get together in public libraries, classrooms, and sometimes even in living rooms. At the end of the evening, they vote for their party's presidential nominee. The candidate who carries the most caucuses is the statewide winner.

While Iowa's caucus tradition dates back to 1846, it only began drawing national and international attention in the 1970s. Candi-

If you want to run for president, Iowa at caucus time is the place to be. Here, Senator Phil Gramm of Texas, vying for the 1996 Republican presidential nomination, greets his supporters at a rally in Davenport.

dates who did well in Iowa's caucuses, such as Jimmy Carter, became their party's national candidates.

As the first presidential primary, the Iowa caucuses winnow out weaker candidates. In 1996, Republican presidential candidate Steve Forbes made a poor showing in the Iowa caucuses. This was a major factor in convincing him to drop out of the race for his party's nomination.

Some people think a state as small as Iowa should not have such a large influence on national issues. They say Iowa's overwhelmingly white population does not represent the country's racial diversity. A spokesperson for the Iowa Caucus Project responds,

"Iowa is sophisticated. A candidate won't win Iowa with a 30-second television spot."

A British journalist adds that the caucuses are "the one stretch on the road to nomination where live candidates consistently face live people, and must persuade them literally to stand up and be counted."

CHILDREN'S ISSUES

Iowa has a long record of looking out for kids' interests. It was among the first states to pass laws regulating child labor, back in the 1890s. More recently, Iowa set up a child abuse registry. This list contains names of adults reported for abusing or neglecting children.

Most children in Iowa have access to a good education. In 1839, the first law the territorial legislature passed was to establish a system of public schools. Because Iowa's population was mostly rural, the one-room schoolhouse became a standard feature of the landscape. By 1937, there were more than nine thousand of them.

Inside these plain white buildings one teacher educated ten to twenty children from all grades. Gradually, Iowans realized that their beloved country schools could not provide the best education. The one-room schools were consolidated into larger school districts. Farm children began boarding buses for new buildings, which had teachers who taught a wider range of subjects. The last one-room schools closed in the mid-1960s.

Iowans are justly proud of their record in education. Nearly 99 percent of adults can read—the highest literacy rate in the nation.

Almost 90 percent of Iowans graduate from high school, and the scores students earn on college admissions tests are well above the national average. The recently established Iowa Communications Network (ICN) will soon give every Iowa classroom access to online interactive instruction.

But Iowa's public schools face challenges in maintaining their reputation. School budgets are tight. Des Moines's thirty-two thousand students attend schools with crumbling roofs and other maintenance problems. Voters there have rejected tax increases that would finance basic repairs.

In Cedar Rapids, students worry that their schools' award-winning music program will be the first target of budget cuts. One parent warns, "We must be constantly alert to make sure that we

Since Iowa's one-room schoolhouses closed, writes historian Joseph Wall, "the bright-yellow school bus . . . has been the most conspicuous vehicle on Iowa country roads."

do not lose the programs that make our public schools the best in the nation and world, programs that fill our lives with music and creativity."

Fortunately, Cedar Rapids schools can draw on community resources to maintain the quality of education. The Symphony School, founded a decade ago, is a joint project of the public schools and the respected Cedar Rapids Symphony. Symphony members add to their salaries by teaching music classes and private lessons, and students receive vouchers for symphony tickets.

CRIME AND PUNISHMENT

Iowa's violent crime rate is only half the national average. Many Iowans recall leaving doors unlocked when they grew up. But recent years have seen an increase in illegal drug use, especially methamphetamine, a stimulant that can be highly addictive. In less than one year, the use of "crank" doubled.

How the state should deal with violent offenders causes much debate among Iowans. Some state legislators have introduced bills to reinstate the death penalty, which was repealed in 1965. Their efforts were supported by Governor Terry Branstad.

State representative Minnette Doderer of Iowa City has worked hard to defeat these measures. "We managed to educate people that it wasn't a solution," Doderer says. "Iowa has one of the lowest murder rates, so why should we have a death penalty?"

For the time being, Iowa remains one of twelve states that do not permit capital punishment. But Iowa's debate over the death penalty is far from decided.

STAYING ON THE FARM

Iowa's greatest natural resource is its farmland. Farmers improve on this built-in advantage by relying on sophisticated machinery to plow, plant, and harvest their crops. The 1920s saw the introduction of hybrid corn, the vigorous, high-yielding plants that resulted from breeding (or "crossing") two species of corn. By the 1950s, almost all farmers had adopted hybrid seed, and the state's cornfields produced an amazing one billion bushels a year.

Today, Iowa is among the leading states in growing corn, hay, and oats. Its soybean production is exceeded only by neighboring

Modern Iowa farmers are as knowledgeable about farm machinery as they are about crops and livestock.

Iowa produces more pigs than any other state.

Illinois, and it is also a major beef producer. Iowa far surpasses all other states in raising pigs: its farmers provide one-fourth of the nation's yearly total. Statistics like these underlie the saying that "the letters I-O-W-A spell corn, and the letters C-O-R-N spell hogs!"

While farm production remains steady, it has become very difficult for small farmers to succeed. During the 1970s, high prices for farm produce caused land prices in Iowa to skyrocket. Then, almost as quickly, produce prices fell again. A U.S. embargo that forbid farmers to export their grain to the Soviet Union made the situation even worse.

RECIPE: CORN COB JELLY

Iowa produces more than one billion bushels of corn each year. The state's thrifty cooks have devised a tasty way of using the cobs that remain after the kernels are stripped off.

To make corn cob jelly, first toss aside cobs that have blemishes or evidence of insects. Take fifteen clean, fresh corn cobs. Boil them in three quarts of water for 90 minutes, and then strain (ask a grown-up to help you).

Add a package of pectin to the three cups of juice that remain. Bring the mixture to a boil, then add three cups of sugar and boil hard for two to three minutes. Pour the jelly into clean glasses and put a layer of melted paraffin on top; let jell.

Spread on toast or a peanut-butter sandwich—and enjoy it!

EARNING A LIVING

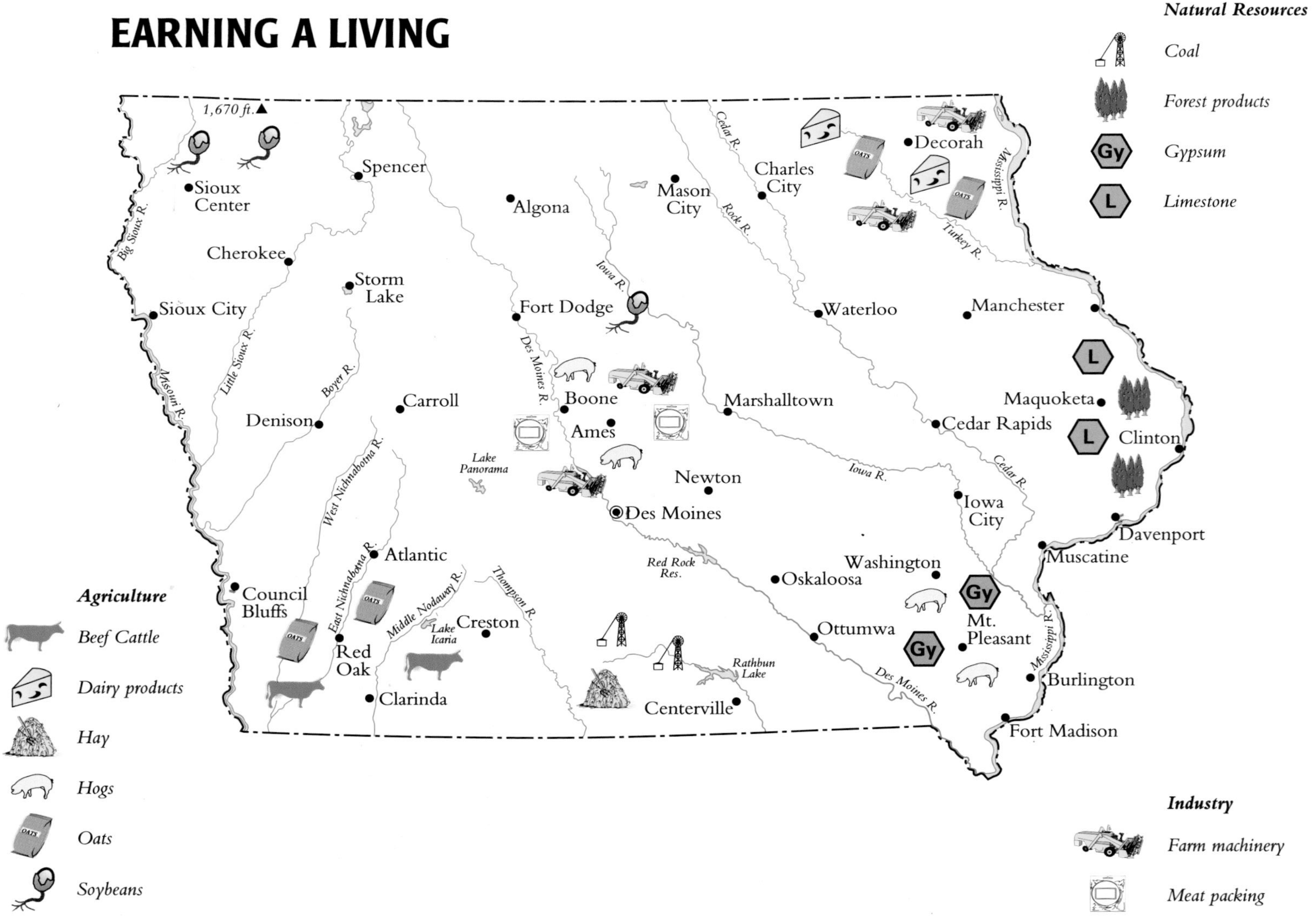

Natural Resources

Coal

Forest products

Gy Gypsum

L Limestone

Industry

Farm machinery

Meat packing

Agriculture

Beef Cattle

Dairy products

Hay

Hogs

Oats

Soybeans

As prices fell, farmers who had borrowed to expand their farms were saddled with enormous debts. Many lost their holdings. From 1982 to 1992, nearly one in six Iowa farmers left the land.

Those who stayed have adapted to new conditions. They must study national and international markets, track the weather, and experiment with new farming methods.

Dave Pepper believes that a good education is a crucial starting point for young farmers. He started pursuing his dream of farming while studying agriculture at Iowa State University in Ames. Today, he farms nearly nine hundred acres near Boone, in the center of the state.

He works long hours and uses old equipment that he repairs himself. His wife, Mary, helps by holding a job in town. After years of effort, they feel their hard work has finally paid off; they even managed to buy the eighty-acre farm Dave's parents had lost in the early 1980s. "I just never wanted to do anything else," Dave

1992 GROSS STATE PRODUCT: $59.2 BILLION

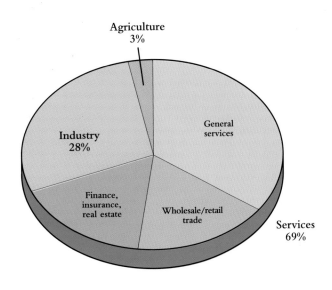

Agriculture 3%

General services

Industry 28%

Finance, insurance, real estate

Wholesale/retail trade

Services 69%

says. "Even at sixteen, I worked three days at a grocery store and quit. I wanted to work on a farm."

In the late 1990s, prices for Iowa farmland began rising again. One reason was an increase in farm prices. Another was the growth of subdivisions and urban development on farmland near cities.

Near Urbandale, an expanding Des Moines suburb, a real estate agency purchased Ernie Thomas's 170-acre farm. Thomas understands that some people would prefer to live in the country—but he hates seeing concrete poured over rich soil. "The rolling unproductive land is where the houses should be, and seeing the good

Farming in Iowa is a family affair.

A GREAT STATE FAIR

Part carnival, part livestock show, the Iowa State Fair is an "ag-extravaganza." For eleven days in August, thousands of fair goers from across the Midwest and beyond roam the Des Moines Fair grounds. Their options range from viewing the Monster Arm Wrestling competition to admiring the award-winning animals displayed on Blue Ribbon Row.

Many people consider Iowa's version the model for all state fairs. The event dates back to 1854, when it began as a small agricultural show in Fairfield. Since then, Iowa's fair has inspired a novel, three movies, and a stage musical.

Since 1960, Norma Duffield Lyon of Toledo has created one of the fair's trademarks, a life-sized cow made of butter. In 1996, she marked Iowa's 150th birthday with a three-dimensional butter sculpture of Iowan Grant Wood's most famous painting, *American Gothic.*

land disappear just eats away at me," he says. "I don't think I'll ever get used to it."

INDUSTRY AND INVENTIONS

Mining, commercial fishing in the Mississippi and Missouri Rivers, and timber production also contribute to Iowa's economy. Iowa ranks third among the states in production of gypsum, a mineral used for construction materials like cement, plasterboard, and tile.

Each year, manufacturing plays an ever-larger role in Iowa's economy. In 1994, for the first time, Iowa's industrial exports had greater value than its farm products. Not surprisingly, much of the state's industry is tied to manufacturing farm equipment or to processing food.

Factories are found throughout the state. In Cedar Rapids, Quaker Oats operates the biggest cereal plant in the country. Sioux City, Waterloo, and Ottumwa are meatpacking centers.

Iowa's homegrown inventors have contributed to their state's economic progress. In Newton in the 1890s, a young man named Fred Maytag tinkered with the crude washing machines of his time, adding gasoline motors. His improvements were an immediate success. Women everywhere were freed from the drudgery of scrub boards and washtubs, and the Maytag Company is now one of Iowa's largest employers.

Des Moines, Iowa's capital and largest city, is a hub for professional and service jobs as well as manufacturing. Many residents hold jobs in state government. Others are employed by the dozens of large insurance companies headquartered there. The printing and publishing industries are also major employers.

COMPANY TOWN ON THE PRAIRIE

At the turn of the century, Iowa had a thriving coal industry. When one coal-mining company faced a shortage of workers, it recruited African-American miners from Southern states. To house them, it built a new town, Buxton, in south-central Monroe County.

Buxton soon grew to six thousand people, most of them African Americans. Workers received housing and medical care. The company even built an auditorium, where touring musicians such as W. C. Handy played Dixieland jazz and Southern blues.

Around 1915, Buxton's coal supply began to give out. The mines closed and the population drifted away. For decades, former townspeople held an annual picnic on the land where Buxton stood.

Today, the only reminders of "the most notable black company town in the country" are a few scars on the open fields.

LOOKING TOWARD THE FUTURE

During the farm depression of the 1980s, many of Iowa's young people left the state, seeking jobs and better futures elsewhere. But in the 1990s, Iowa's economy and spirits are rising. The state actively recruits new businesses. New jobs have resulted in the third-lowest unemployment rate in the country.

In his 1997 Condition of the State message, Governor Branstad voiced Iowa's optimistic mood. "We have already turned the corner in Iowa," he said. "From recovery to growth, from scraping by to building reserves, this state is poised for great things to come. Iowa is a work in progress."

4 ORDINARY IOWANS

In the 1989 movie *Field of Dreams*, the ghost of an old-time baseball player returns to earth. He lands in the middle of a cornfield. "Is this heaven?" the player asks, gazing around in wonder.

The answer: "No. It's Iowa."

Few Iowans would boast that their state is heavenly, but many agree that it has special qualities. It preserves its folk traditions, such as 114 home remedies for warts (one is to rub your wart when you see a stranger and say, "Take it, stranger"). Yet modern Iowa also embraces high-tech innovations like genetically engineered soybeans and fiber optics.

SMALL TOWNS

With 2,840,000 people, Iowa ranks thirtieth among the states in population. Most people live in the southeastern quadrant of the state, but even that area is not densely populated. Resources are distributed fairly equally across the state, with rich farmland found nearly everywhere. As a result, no single region dominates the others.

Unlike neighboring Illinois, Iowa lacks a sprawling metropolitan area. Approximately 400,000 people live in the greater Des Moines area. The state's other main urban areas are Cedar Rapids, Davenport, and Sioux City.

Though it has no big cities, Iowa has many small ones: the state contains 950 incorporated cities. Some people think that small-town life defines the character of Iowa and Iowans.

"Iowa has always had a small-town ethos," says an editor of two small Iowa newspapers. "All those qualities that most people associate with rural life and small communities, like openness and trust and a willingness to bend over backward to help others, are still valued here."

The residents of Iowa's small communities tend to be boosters.

TEN LARGEST CITIES

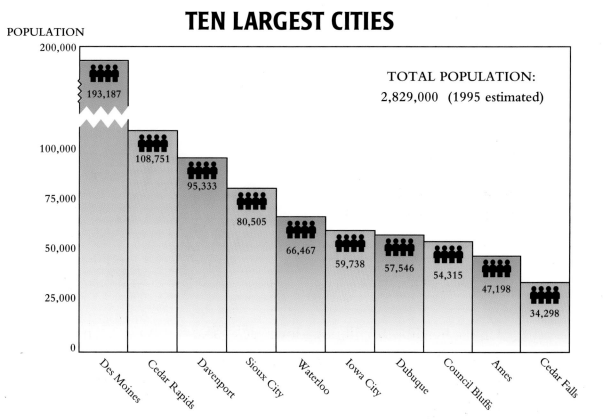

POPULATION

TOTAL POPULATION: 2,829,000 (1995 estimated)

200,000

193,187

100,000

108,751

95,333

75,000

80,505

66,467

50,000

59,738

57,546

54,315

47,198

25,000

34,298

0

Des Moines | Cedar Rapids | Davenport | Sioux City | Waterloo | Iowa City | Dubuque | Council Bluffs | Ames | Cedar Falls

They are proud of their environment and seek to share it with others. Billboards across the state welcome visitors to each new town: "Jewel, a Gem in a Friendly Setting" or "Welcome Stranger to Friendly Granger." With the rise of the Internet, some towns have gone online to attract industries and newcomers. Check out cyberspace to find Manly ("A Great Place with Great Expectations") and Osage ("The Small Community with a Big Difference").

People who grew up in small-town Iowa have divided opinions about it. Some of Iowa's best writers, such as Ruth Suckow, depicted the state's hamlets as closed societies in which everyone thought alike. For others, small towns represent havens, where

4-H clubs are an important activity for Iowa's small-town kids.

you can know your neighbors and avoid the rush and danger of cities.

In her memoir, *Blooming: A Small Town Girlhood*, Susan Allen Toth fondly recalled her 1950s childhood in Ames. She and her friends grew up "quietly," she wrote. "We were not seared by fierce poverty, racial tensions, drug abuse, street crime."

An Iowa-born journalist paints a different picture. "Small-town life isn't quite as calm as everybody likes to romanticize it," she says. "It's not always a happy little life on the farm. It's a myth that Iowans have no problems."

LOSING POPULATION

During the 1980s, Iowa's way of life lost some of its appeal. By the end of the decade, there were two hundred thousand fewer Iowans than in 1980. Part of the population decline was caused by an agricultural depression. Prices for produce collapsed, and many farmers lost their land. A severe drought in 1988 intensified farmers' problems. Young people, especially college graduates, fled the state to find jobs and new experiences elsewhere.

In the 1990s, the trend has reversed. Farm prices are booming again. Unemployment in Iowa is extremely low. One major moving company claims that for the past three years in a row more moving vans have entered Iowa than have left it. Figures showing a small population increase support this assertion.

Many Iowans have made a commitment to preserve their unique way of life. One such person is Debra Norman, a farmer and businesswoman from Decatur City. Norman juggles work, family, and

Historian Joseph Wall called Iowa a state of small towns, "where all of our cities are in reality small towns grown somewhat larger." Here, townspeople gather on Main Street in Moscow, Iowa.

an assortment of volunteer projects aimed at keeping small-town main streets alive.

Norman believes that townspeople and farmers are each other's natural allies. If families stay on the farm, small-town businesses will prosper. She explains, "A lot of my background is in living on the farm but working in town. A lot of my volunteer work is in programs to bring the two together."

"In a small town," she adds, "even one person can make a difference."

A MIX OF PEOPLES

Nearly 97 percent of Iowans are white. They are descendants of pioneers or the thousands of immigrants who flocked to the state in the mid-nineteenth century. About one in five Iowans has a German ancestor. Other immigrants came in waves from England, Ireland, Norway, Sweden, Bohemia, Holland, and Denmark. All followed the writer Horace Greeley's advice to go west to the "land of the unhidden sky."

Iowa's communities preserve their ethnic ties in many ways. In Pella, which was settled by Dutch immigrants, kids get their

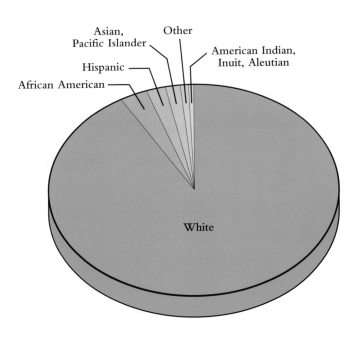

ETHNIC IOWA

Asian, Pacific Islander

Other

Hispanic

American Indian, Inuit, Aleutian

African American

White

Christmas presents early: December 5 is Sinter Klaas (Santa Claus) Day, when Saint Nicholas and his servants arrive to hand out gifts. Pella also celebrates its Dutch heritage with a Tulip Festival, a reminder of the Netherlands's fame for growing tulips. During this time, the town's gardens bloom with acres of the vivid flowers, and families don Dutch costumes, complete with wooden shoes.

Decorah, in northeastern Iowa, preserves its Norwegian flavor in the Vesterheim (which means "western home"), one of the oldest and largest immigrant museums in the country. The museum buildings date from the town's days as a gateway for Norwegian settlers stream-

Residents of Pella wear traditional Dutch garb for the town's yearly Tulip Festival.

ing into the American West. On the other side of the state, Kimballton honors its Danish settlers by flying the U.S. and Danish flags side by side, while nearby Elk Horn boasts a windmill that was transported in thirty thousand pieces from Denmark and then reassembled.

Iowa's small African-American population (less than 2 percent) is concentrated in the cities, particularly Des Moines and Sioux City. The few blacks who came to Iowa in the nineteenth century often worked in the river towns of Keokuk, Burlington, and Muscatine. Others were brought in as strikebreakers in the coal mines of southern Iowa.

Sixty years before universities in the South were forcibly integrated, the great botanist George Washington Carver completed his studies at Iowa State College (now Iowa State University). Carver had been born a slave in Missouri.

By 1870, strict laws in Iowa prohibited segregation of the races. Even steamboats passing through the state's waters were forbidden to allow segregation.

In practice, incidents of racism occurred in Iowa. Yet its many advances caused President Ulysses S. Grant to call the state "the nation's one bright radical star."

Iowa's African-American community has played a role in state events well beyond its small size. Iowa's public schools were integrated in 1868, when the state supreme court ruled that Susan Clark could attend Muscatine's public schools. The suit was brought by her father, a former slave who became a lawyer. In Des Moines, an African-American newspaper, the *Iowa State Bystander*, was published from 1894 until the mid-1980s.

In 1995, LaMetta K. Wynn made Iowa history by being elected

When LaMetta K. Wynn was elected mayor of Clinton in 1995, she made Iowa history by being the first black woman to become mayor of an Iowa town.

mayor of Clinton, a city on the Mississippi River. She was the first black woman to become the mayor of an Iowa town.

Iowa was once home to about twenty Native American tribes. Now there is one. In the 1850s, a group of Mesquakie who had been put on a Kansas reservation resolved to return to their beloved Iowa. Using annuity payments they had received for moving to Kansas, they purchased eighty acres of land near the present town of Tama—paying six times the going rate for white settlers.

For ten years, the Indians crowded onto their small plot, facing near starvation. They could buy no more land to hunt or raise crops on, because the federal government had cut off their annuities.

Finally, in 1866, the United States secretary of the interior—an Iowan himself—reinstated the payments. The Mesquakie then acquired a total of three thousand acres. Six thousand of their descendants remain there.

NEWCOMERS

Some of the newest Iowans belong to the state's Hispanic community, which is thirty thousand strong and growing. The first Hispanics arrived in the 1930s to work in the sugar beet fields. More recently, they have settled in urban areas like Sioux City, Waterloo, and Cedar Rapids. Many have jobs in the meatpacking industry.

Some residents of the Mesquakie Tribal Settlement near Tama celebrate their heritage by practicing traditional crafts such as beadwork.

Mexican Americans living in Iowa preserve their cultural traditions, such as this folklórico *dance.*

The latest group to settle in Iowa are Bosnian refugees. In 1996, forty-seven Bosnian refugees took jobs at Waterloo's IBP meat-packing plant. Like thousands of immigrants before them, the Bosnians are very glad to have reached Iowa. "They hope to make it their home," says Almir Pajazetovic, the group's spokesperson.

THE PRAIRIE ROSE

The Winnebago Indians were a prairie people who lived in Iowa in the 1840s. After a few years, the U.S. Army moved them out of the state. This Winnebago folktale explains the origin of Iowa's state flower, the wild rose.

Long ago, no flowers bloomed on the prairie. The Earth Mother felt very sad when she looked upon her robe of dull shrubs and green grasses.

But Earth had many flowers in her heart. One by one, these flowers went out and tried to live upon the prairie. But, each time, the Wind Demon rushed at them and blew out their lives. At last, the Prairie Rose offered to go and bloom upon the colorless prairie.

As before, the Wind Demon ran after Prairie Rose. He meant to kill her, too. But when he drew closer, he was charmed by her wonderful fragrance.

So the Wind Demon allowed the Prairie Rose to live. Soon he changed and became quiet. He sent gentle breezes over the prairie grasses. The other flowers came up from the heart of the Earth Mother, and her robe became beautiful.

Sometimes the Wind becomes loud and noisy. But his loudness does not last long. And he does not harm a person whose robe is the color of Prairie Rose.

SPORTS

Iowa has no major-league sports teams, but residents make up for this by passionately following college and high school sports of all kinds. University of Iowa fans focus their attention on the exploits of their beloved Hawkeyes, who play in the tough Big Ten athletic conference. In small towns, everyone tracks the progress of their high school heroes on the gridiron, baseball field, and basketball court.

Girls' sports draw their share of the attention. The popularity of Iowa girls' basketball has even been recognized by the Smithsonian Institution in Washington, D.C. During the summer of 1996, the Smithsonian featured Iowa in its annual Festival of American Folklife. More than a million tourists viewed exhibits on the state, as well as polka lessons, instructions on tractor building, and a demonstration by talented girls' basketball teams.

RELIGION AND IDEALS

Iowa's first church was built by Methodists in 1834, just two years after the territory opened for settlement. Since then Iowans have followed a variety of religious traditions.

In the 1840s, Methodist "circuit riders" traveled from town to town, preaching the gospel and conducting marriages and funerals. Thanks to their efforts, Methodism had the largest number of converts in the state.

Kalona, eighteen miles north of Iowa City, was settled by Amish and Mennonite immigrants, who had been persecuted in Germany and Switzerland for their religious beliefs. Kalona's Old Order Amish still live a simple farming life, shunning cars, telephones, and electricity.

During frontier days, Iowa's empty prairies appealed to people who wanted to build a different kind of community, called a utopia. Iowa's utopias were based on their founders' ideas for a perfect

WHEELING IT IN IOWA

Iowa's gently rolling terrain is ideal for bicycling, and many Iowans love to take to two wheels. Each spring and summer, towns and counties across the state sponsor dozens of races, ranging from the Tour de Poweshiek (in Poweshiek County) to the Snake Alley Criterium in Burlington.

The biggest race of all is RAGBRAI, the (Des Moines) Register's Annual Great Bicycle Ride Across Iowa. This five-day event attracts thousands of contestants, some from other countries.

Actor Tom Arnold, a native Iowan, rode in the 1996 RAGBRAI with a group of his friends from his Ottumwa high school. Their team had the same name as the band they had belonged to in high school: the Massive Fergusons.

society. These included owning all property in common. Some groups also supported the radical notion of equal rights for women.

Towns with names like Icaria, Salubria, and Communia rose from the prairies, but most lasted only a few years. Their members squabbled and broke into competing factions. After a while they drifted back east, or to Europe or California.

Iowa's only successful experiment in communal living was the Amana Colonies. The Community of True Inspiration, a German

A blacksmith plies his trade in the Amana Colonies, where residents still practice a variety of handicrafts.

religious group, built seven villages on twenty-six thousand acres of rich farmland. They owned their lands together and ate in common dining rooms.

For ninety years, Amana prospered. But gradually, the colonies' young people began leaving. They took jobs in Iowa City and Des Moines; then they came home to show off their new cars and persuade their friends to come away with them. Finally, in 1932, the villagers voted to dissolve their communal way of life.

Despite their short existence, the utopian communities made a difference in Iowa. The groups' biggest contribution, says historian Joseph Wall, was bringing in fresh ideas. They gave Iowa "a much-needed ideological diversity."

The town of Corning, near the site of Icaria, which was founded by French settlers in the 1850s, celebrates with a *festival de l'héritage français* (French Heritage Festival). The event features a parade, tours of the site, and—just for fun—a French poodle contest.

THE IOWA WALTZ

Iowa has strong musical traditions that have their roots in the nineteenth century. The first pioneers brought with them both their folk music and a love of singing. On Thursday nights after cornhusking season ended, young people from miles around went to "singing schools," where they learned their notes and scales from the "singing professor."

Iowa's settlers also established the "barn dance," which was originally held to celebrate the building of a house or raising of a barn. Pretty soon people stopped waiting for special occasions. Barn dances became events in themselves.

Folk music still thrives in Iowa, at square dances, at coffeehouses, and in schools. The 1996 Festival of Iowa Folklife featured master Iowa fiddler Al Murphy and his Harvest Home ensemble playing "The Iowa Waltz."

FOLK ARTISTS AND CRAFTSPEOPLE

From furniture making to Easter egg painting to quilting, Iowa's handicraft traditions remain strong. The first quilts were household necessities in a land with bitter winters. But they also gave their creators an opportunity to express themselves artistically, and quilting bees provided welcome social occasions for isolated pioneer women. Today, collectors prize older or antique quilts, especially those created by the Amish settlers.

There has also been a rebirth of interest in fashioning these beautiful heirlooms. Leona Hershberger of Kalona took up quilting after retiring from the banking industry. She pieces together about one quilt a month. "At one time I almost thought it was a lost art, but I think it's coming back. The young people are picking it up," she says.

Marjorie Nejdl is the artist-in-residence at Cedar Rapids's National Czech and Slovak Museum and Library. Using beeswax and dyes, she creates colorful Easter eggs, each one a unique work of art. "I learned to do this as a child from my uncle and my mother," she says. "It was part of my heritage."

The state's crafts held such an allure for one Iowa woman that she opened a store specializing in them. Her small boutique is located not in Ames, her hometown, but in Houston, Texas, where she has lived for fourteen years.

The store owner proudly answers questions about her wares. There are Amish quilts dating from the 1930s; handwoven baskets from the Amana Colonies; and wooden cabinets painted in cheerful colors and fanciful designs. As she talks, it becomes clear why she has recreated a little bit of her native state in the Southwest.

"I love Iowa," she admits. "I miss it."

Artist Marjorie Nejdl draws on her Czech heritage to create decorative eggs.

5 MAKING A MARK

In 1959, the premier of the then Soviet Union dropped in on Roswell Garst's farm near Coon Rapids. Surrounded by reporters and Secret Service agents, Nikita Khrushchev was a man on a mission. He wanted to see Iowa's incredibly productive farms for himself.

Forty years later, most people recognize that the state's rich soil sprouts more than corn. Iowa has made great advances in agriculture, but it has also produced an abundance of artists, writers, scientists, and musicians.

IMPROVING ON NATURE

The productive fields that awed Khrushchev owe much to the development of hybrid corn. The Iowan who did most to popularize hybrid seed was Henry A. Wallace.

Born into a prominent Iowa family, Wallace was a student of George Washington Carver's at Iowa State University. There he became interested in genetics: crossing, or breeding, two plants to create a stronger, more productive species. In the 1920s, he cofounded the Pioneer Seed Corn Company, which brought hybrid seed into the commercial market. In 1932, less than 1 percent of Iowa farmers had tried out the newfangled seed. By 1944, nearly 100 percent of them were using it, and corn yields had risen by half.

Nikita Khrushchev, premier of the then Soviet Union, visited the United States in 1959. Near the top of his agenda was touring this Iowa farm outside Coon Rapids.

Iowan Henry A. Wallace, the secretary of agriculture during the Great Depression, did much to improve the farmer's lot.

In 1933, Wallace was appointed secretary of agriculture by President Franklin Delano Roosevelt. It was the Great Depression. The country was in the grip of hard times, and farmers were especially hard hit.

Wallace served as a prime architect of Roosevelt's New Deal, which established government programs to provide relief from the depression. He also fought for farmers' rights. He helped institute measures such as paying farmers to limit their production (in order to raise prices to a fair level) and bringing electricity to rural areas. His legacy also includes the first soil conservation programs. After serving one term as Roosevelt's vice president, Wallace ran unsuccessfully for president in 1948 as leader of the Progressive Party.

Another agricultural innovator was Cresco native Norman Borlaug, whose research helped impoverished farmers feed their families. Borlaug worked to develop wheat seeds that could be grown in the warm climates of developing countries. Bigger wheat harvests helped Mexico become a food exporter and averted famine in India and Pakistan. In 1970, Borlaug received the Nobel Peace Prize for his role in what is called the Green Revolution.

INVENTIVE IOWANS

Iowa researchers helped usher in the computer age. John Vincent Atanasoff was an Iowa State University professor. In 1939, he and one of his graduate students, Clifford Berry, created the first electronic digital computer. A few years later World War II broke out, and Atanasoff went off to Washington, D.C., to work for

John Vincent Atanasoff was coinventor of the first modern digital computer. Atanasoff and an engineering student, Clifford Berry, built the device in 1939 but did not receive credit for their discovery until 1973.

the government. His breakthrough invention was forgotten. In the meantime, other researchers used some of Atanasoff's ideas to design their own computer.

In 1973, Atanasoff and Berry finally received credit for constructing the first digital computer. Currently, a laboratory at Iowa State is trying to build a replica of the original machine.

Perhaps Iowa's most prominent scientist is James Van Allen, a physicist at the University of Iowa. In 1958, Van Allen and his research team built *Explorer I*, the first satellite successfully launched by the United States. *Explorer I* carried a device designed to detect cosmic rays—high energy particles from distant space. The device confirmed Van Allen's prediction that the earth was

Physicist James Van Allen (third from left) is Iowa's most prominent scientist and the discoverer of the Van Allen radiation belts—streams of charged particles trapped in the earth's magnetic field.

encircled by two belts of protective radiation. The larger of these Van Allen belts (named for their discoverer) extends forty thousand miles above the earth. Van Allen still works in his University of Iowa lab.

A JAZZ STAR

Each year in July, thousands of jazz fans converge on Davenport, hometown of Leon "Bix" Beiderbecke. The throngs arrive from as close by as Illinois and as far away as Italy. Their ultimate destination is the Bix Beiderbecke Memorial Jazz Festival, which features three days of toe-tapping music by top jazz bands.

TURNING ON THE LIGHTS

Imagine doing your homework by kerosene light. Consider having no refrigerator to raid. Life without electricity seems more typical of the last century than this one. But only sixty years ago, nine out of ten Iowa farms relied on gaslights, kerosene, and candles. Thick slabs of ice cooled their "ice boxes."

In 1930s Iowa, farmers could not believe that the Rural Electrification Administration, or REA, would actually work. They thought "it was all some kind of hoax," writes Carl Hamilton, an Iowan who worked in the REA.

Yet the success of the program literally turned on the lights, in farms across Iowa and everywhere else. "Rural electrification did more to change rural America than any other single thing," says Hamilton.

Born in 1903, Bix started his music studies early. A friend recalls that "Bix was the best piano player in his kindergarten class." By the age of sixteen, he was playing jazz cornet on Mississippi riverboats. When Bix was eighteen, his parents sent him to Lake Forest Military Academy near Chicago. They hoped to direct his attention away from music and toward his studies. No luck. The city's flourishing jazz scene drew the young musician in.

Soon he left Lake Forest and began playing gigs in and around Chicago. For the next seven years, he toured nationally with the best-known big bands of his era. Bix was a brilliant improviser, weaving intricate riffs with his cornet. He also composed many jazz piano pieces that have become classics, such as "In a Mist," "In the Dark," and "Candlelights."

One of Bix's mentors was renowned trumpet player Louis

Cornet player Bix Beiderbecke (second from right) influenced the jazz artists of his day and beyond. Each year, the Bix Beiderbecke Memorial Society and his hometown of Davenport host a music festival in his honor.

Armstrong. In turn, Bix inspired famous musicians of his day, like Hoagy Carmichael. He even influenced the modern jazz icon Miles Davis.

Tragically, Bix Beiderbecke's career and life were cut short by alcoholism. After Bix died, at age twenty-eight, Louis Armstrong said, "If that boy had lived, he'd be the greatest."

A MIDWESTERN ARTIST

In August 1930, a little-known Iowa painter named Grant Wood visited Eldon, a small town in southern Iowa. There he happened upon a house he liked: a simple frame building with a Gothic-style window in its gable. The house made such an impression that Wood used it as the backdrop for a painting.

Wood asked Dr. B. H. McKeeby, a dentist from Cedar Rapids, to pose as a stern farmer holding a pitchfork. Grant's own sister, Nan, played the role of the farmer's daughter. Both models wore clothes like those Wood had seen in old photographs in his own family album.

When *American Gothic* was finished, Wood sent it to an exhibition of American paintings and sculpture at the Art Institute of Chicago. To his amazement, the painting won a bronze medal and a three-hundred-dollar prize. It became famous not only in Chicago, but around the world.

Today, the painting of the serious, silent farmers still hangs in Chicago's Art Institute. For its many admirers, the work symbolizes the down-to-earth spirit of the American Midwest.

Wood made his reputation with *American Gothic*, but the Anamosa native had spent years studying and perfecting his craft. He developed a unique style, combining a realistic approach with techniques from folk art.

Some of his paintings poked fun at American traditions, such as the legend of George Washington and the cherry tree. This story was actually invented by a clergyman named Mason Weems. Wood's painting is called *Parson Weems' Fable*. It shows an adult head of George Washington placed on a six-year-old's body; the small figure waves an ax before a cherry tree.

For many people, Wood's scenes of the Iowa countryside capture the essence of the state. Historian Joseph Wall claims that when

Artist Grant Wood was born into a farm family in Anamosa. One critic wrote that "his pioneer background is evident in the patient, meticulous, and somewhat rigid craftsmanship shown in his work."

Wood painted American Gothic, his most famous work, over a two-month period in 1930.

New Yorkers whiz through the state on Interstate 80, they glance out the window and exclaim, "Why, it looks just like a Grant Wood painting!"

In 1996, the U.S. Postal Service chose a Grant Wood print—*Young Corn, 1931*—for the official Iowa statehood stamp. Some Iowans were disappointed. They hoped that a high-tech scene would be selected, showcasing Iowa's scientific contributions. Many others disagreed.

"I think this depicts Iowa, the beauty of Iowa, and that which people all around the world would love to share and be a part of," said Robert Ray, former governor of the state.

WRITERS

Iowa's vast prairies and hard-working people have inspired many writers. At first, writers from Iowa felt they had to leave the farms and villages where they had grown up. They moved to big cities, like Chicago, Boston, and New York, to compose works about life on the Midwestern prairies.

One such exile was Hamlin Garland. As a boy in Mitchell County in the 1860s and 1870s, Garland performed endless rounds of chores on his parents' farm. He hated his tasks of plowing and sowing as much as he loved Iowa's natural beauty.

Garland's many novels, stories, and essays include *Main-Travelled Roads, Prairie Folk,* and *Wayside Courtships*. All show a mixed attitude: awe for the grandeur of Iowa's prairies combined with sympathy for what Garland considered the "grim plight" of rural Iowans, especially women.

Hamlin Garland has been called "the first actual farmer in American fiction." He wrote realistic stories and novels about the hardships of rural midwestern life.

In his 1917 autobiography, *Son of the Middle Border*, Garland described his homesteading childhood. He also argued that Iowa must create a literature of its own: "Why has this land no storytellers like those who have made Massachusetts and New Hampshire illustrious?"

Long before Garland's death, Iowa began developing homegrown "storytellers." One of the most notable was Ruth Suckow. Like Garland, she wrote about small-town and farm life. Her novels *Country People* and *The Folks* gained her fame in the 1920s and 1930s.

Suckow was the daughter of a minister. She did most of her writing in New York's Greenwich Village but kept the Iowa connections that fed her work. During the summer, she lived in the town of Earlville, in eastern Iowa. Town residents grew accustomed to seeing her ride her bicycle between her two-room cottage and the beehives she tended, wearing her trademark attire of knee-length knickers.

Contemporary writer Jane Smiley belongs to the line of Iowa authors who use rural life as the backdrop for their stories. Smiley won a Pulitzer Prize in 1992 for her novel *A Thousand Acres*. Set on an Iowa farm, the account of a farmer and his troubled relationships with his daughters is modeled on *King Lear*, a tragic play by William Shakespeare.

The University of Iowa in Iowa City has welcomed aspiring and established writers for eighty years. After World War II, the University of Iowa's Writers' Workshop was established. Paul Engle, a well-known Iowa poet, became the director.

The workshop's two-year program has since gained an international reputation. A selective list of participants reads like a Who's Who of famous American authors. Flannery O'Connor, Raymond Carver, T. Coraghessan Boyle, Tennessee Williams, John Cheever, and John Irving, among many others, either taught or studied at the workshop.

Each year the writers' workshop sponsors a summer festival. In June and July, more than a thousand writers gather in Iowa City. By day, they analyze their own literary efforts; by night, they hear noted writers read and discuss their work.

6 EXPLORING IOWA

Harvest Days, Living History Farms

Asked to name her favorite aspect of Iowa, an Ames woman barely pauses to think. "Oh, the small towns, of course," she says. "They're absolutely pristine."

Over the past decade, Iowa communities have worked hard to spruce up their turn-of-the-century main streets. Quaint shops and old train depots appeal to many visitors. But Iowa has much else to offer. The Hawkeye State abounds with Indian mounds, scenic views, and famous movie sets. The state even boasts some architectural gems.

EFFIGY MOUNDS

Long before Marquette and Jolliet paddled their canoes along the Upper Mississippi River, Native Americans buried their dead on the high bluffs rising above the water. Effigy Mounds National Monument is located in the northwestern corner of the state. Iowa's only national monument, the park contains nearly two hundred prehistoric burial mounds. Twenty-nine take the shape of birds or bears; these distinctive effigies are thought to be at least 1,500 years old.

Nowadays these mounds are steeped in serenity. As you walk along Fire Point Trail, you can almost hear the solemn rituals these

Seen from the air, these distinctive burial mounds at Effigy Mounds National Monument resemble a procession of animals. Their fitting name is the Marching Bear Group.

vanished peoples carried out to determine the shape of the mounds.

LIFE ON THE MISSISSIPPI

In the 1920s, a brash East Coast editor declared that his new magazine, the *New Yorker*, would not be published for "the little old lady from Dubuque."

If 1990s Dubuque residents could answer Harold Ross, they might point out that their handsome town is much more cosmopolitan than he assumed. Steep hills, cable cars, and Victorian houses lend Dubuque some of the charm of San Francisco. A monument marking the grave of Julien Dubuque, the town's namesake, stands just south of the city.

When Dubuque's lead mines were exhausted, the city became a busy lumber town and bustling port. This colorful past is on display in the Mississippi Riverboat Museum. Here you can learn about explorers, pilots, and riverboat gamblers, and board one of the world's last side-wheeled steamboats.

South of Dubuque lies Saint Donatus, which was founded by immigrants from the tiny European nation of Luxembourg. Each

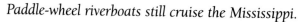

Paddle-wheel riverboats still cruise the Mississippi.

year on Good Friday, hundreds of people wend their way uphill to the Chapel on the Mount, modeled on a chapel in their native country. Saint Donatus is the only surviving Luxembourger community in the United States.

About halfway down Iowa's eastern border, the town of Davenport has preserved its past as a limestone exporter and port in the Putnam Museum, one of the oldest museums west of the Mississippi. East Davenport, the largest historical district in the state, is a charming neighborhood of brick-paved streets and small shops.

The "crookedest street in the world" (according to Ripley's *Believe It or Not)* is a steep, zigzagging road in Burlington. Built in 1893, Snake Alley makes five half-curves and two quarter-curves in just 275 feet. Even the bricks were laid at an angle, to give horses' hooves a better grip on the surface in winter. Every year, determined bicyclists tackle these curves in the Snake Alley Criterium race.

Admirers of Mark Twain will find traces of the great writer's early life in Keokuk. In the mid-1850s, he worked in a print shop here. Some of his possessions can be seen at the restored Miller House and at the Mark Twain Center in the Keokuk Public Library.

EASTERN IOWA

Just outside Dyersville lies one of the world's most famous cornfields. Fans of the movie *Field of Dreams* can play a few innings on the baseball diamond featured in the film. There is even a concession stand.

Readers of Laura Ingalls Wilder's *Little House* books make a

Snake Alley winds its way to the top of a ridge in Burlington. It has been called the "crookedest street in the world."

beeline for the town of Burr Oak. In the 1870s, a plague of grasshoppers destroyed Charles Ingalls's crops in neighboring Minnesota. He moved his family to Burr Oak and, for a year, tried his hand at the hotel business. A guide takes you through the modest eleven-room hotel that the Ingalls girls, Mary and young Laura, helped to run.

About thirty miles west of Burr Oak stands Hayden Prairie. These

PLACES TO SEE

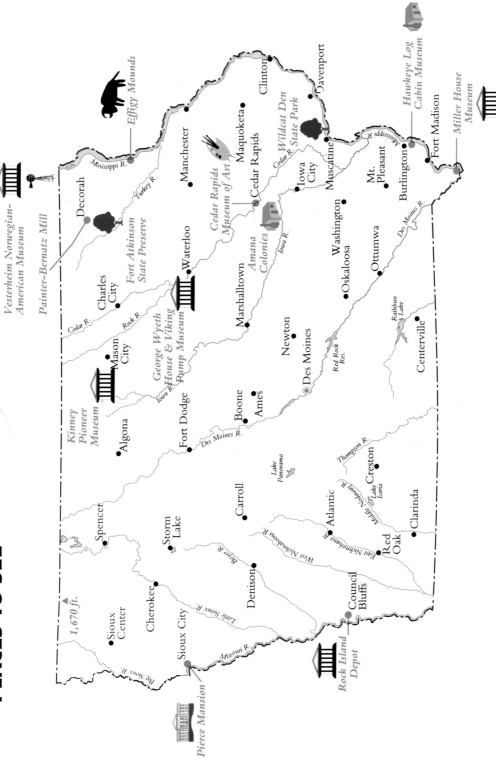

Effigy Mounds

Vesterheim Norwegian–
American Museum

Painter–Bernatz Mill

Fort Atkinson
State Preserve

Decorah

Mississippi R.

Turkey R.

Manchester

Cedar Rapids
Museum of Art

Maquoketa

Cedar Rapids

Clinton

Davenport

Wildcat Den
State Park

Muscatine

Cedar R.

Iowa City

Amana
Colonies

Iowa R.

Washington

Oskaloosa

Ottumwa

Mt.
Pleasant

Burlington

Fort Madison

Hawkeye Log
Cabin Museum

Miller House
Museum

Mississippi R.

Charles
City

Waterloo

George Wyeth
House & Viking
Pump Museum

Marshalltown

Cedar R.

Rock R.

Mason
City

Iowa R.

Kinney
Pioneer
Museum

Algona

Fort Dodge

Boone

Ames

Newton

Des Moines

Red Rock
Res.

Red Rock Res.

Rathbun
Lake

Centerville

Des Moines R.

Des Moines R.

Spencer

Storm
Lake

Carroll

Lake
Panorama

Thompson R.

Creston

Lake
Icaria

Atlantic

Middle Nodaway R.

Clarinda

Red
Oak

East Nishnabotna R.

West Nishnabotna R.

Boyer R.

Denison

Cherokee

Sioux
Center

Sioux City

Little Sioux R.

Big Sioux R.

Missouri R.

Council
Bluffs

Rock Island
Depot

Pierce Mansion

1,670 ft.

THE MORMON CROSSINGS

Southern Iowa still bears the marks of a remarkable human migration. From 1846 to 1856, as many as thirty thousand Mormons crossed the state. Most were on their way to Salt Lake City, Utah.

The Mormons were fleeing from Nauvoo, Illinois, where their leader, John Smith, had been murdered by hostile neighbors.

The first group of emigrants blazed a trail. They established "Camps of Israel" at stopping places, planting gardens and digging wells for the thousands who would follow. Heavy wagon wheels wore the Mormon Trail, which can still be seen from Fort Madison to Council Bluffs.

Some of the crossings took place in howling winter weather. At Mount Pisgah in Union County, eight hundred graves bear silent witness to the travelers' hardships.

The last wave of Mormons crossed Iowa in 1856. One thousand three hundred converts from Europe arrived in Iowa City by train, and continued across the state on foot. Historians call this the Handcart Expedition, because the immigrants pushed their belongings ahead of them in carts.

Some of these pioneers left the trail and settled in south-central Iowa. Graceland College, in Lamoni, was founded by these Mormons, who broke with their leader, Brigham Young.

240 acres comprise one the few native prairies left in the state. Spring and fall, when the wildflowers bloom, are the best times to visit—and to imagine how Iowa looked when 80 percent of it was covered with tallgrass prairie.

In 1893, an American friend of Czech composer Antonín Dvorák persuaded him to move to New York City. Dvorák went, but soon grew homesick for the customs and accents of his native land. He spent the summer of 1893 in tiny Spillville, Iowa, founded by immigrants from the Czech region of Bohemia.

In Spillville, Dvorák polished his most famous work, the symphony *From the New World*. Visitors to Spillville can tour the two-story house where Dvorák resided. Upstairs is a museum dedicated to him. The lower floor houses the Bily Clock Museum, which contains a collection of hand-carved timepieces.

The Czech influence is also strong in Cedar Rapids. For many years, Iowa's second-largest city had the highest percentage of Czech residents of any city in the country.

The wildflower Blazing Star shows its colors in Hayden Prairie, one of the first tallgrass prairies Iowans sought to preserve.

Presidents from three nations attended the dedication of the National Czech and Slovak Museum and Library in Cedar Rapids. Gathered, from left to right, are Michal Kovác (Slovak Republic), Bill Clinton (United States), and Václav Havel (Czech Republic).

In 1995, Cedar Rapids dedicated the National Czech and Slovak Museum and Library. The ceremony brought together the presidents of the United States, the Czech Republic, and the Slovak Republic. "Many of our fellow countrymen eventually settled here in Cedar Rapids," said Czech president Václav Havel. "They came here to Iowa to find freedom, prosperity, and mutual tolerance."

The Cedar Rapids Museum of Art contains the world's largest

THE AMANA COLONIES

The Amana Colonies are seven villages founded by a nineteenth-century Protestant sect called the Community of True Inspiration. They entice tourists with their picturesque buildings, high-quality woolens, and handcrafted goods.

The colonies' large, country-style restaurants serve up hearty home-cooked meals. On weekends, these attract hungry college students from the University of Iowa and Grinnell College.

Serious cooking is a long tradition in the Amana Colonies. Until 1932, the colonies' residents ate all their meals together, in communal dining halls. Each kitchen was run by a *kuchebaas* (kitchen boss). Amana resident Marie Calahan went to work in one of the kitchens in 1928. After two weeks' training, she got up one morning at five o'clock and prepared breakfast for forty people. It was her fourteenth birthday.

When Amana ended its communal way of life, families began eating in their own homes. Nearly fifty head cooks were thrown out of work.

"That's why we have these big restaurants here," explains Emilie Hoppe, author of a cookbook of recipes from the Amana Colonies. "Our restaurants grew out of the communal kitchen heritage."

collection of paintings by artist Grant Wood, who spent most of his adult life in Cedar Rapids. In addition, the museum features many works by Marvin Cone, a lifelong friend of Wood who also painted landscapes of rolling Midwestern farmland.

The gem of the University of Iowa's campus, in Iowa City, is the old capitol building. A journalist for the *Cedar Rapids Gazette* describes the grand limestone edifice, which was completed in 1842, as "a palace fit for presidents." By 1857, the state capital had moved to Des Moines, and the "palace" became university property. Today, visitors enjoy climbing the unusual reverse spiral staircase in the central hall.

West of Iowa City, in the village of West Branch, is a carefully preserved Quaker cottage. This two-room structure is the boyhood home of Herbert Hoover, the only U.S. president born in Iowa. Hoover lived in West Branch until he was ten; after both his parents died, he was sent to Oregon to live with an uncle.

The tranquil grounds of the Herbert Hoover National Historic Site include the Quaker meetinghouse where the Hoover family attended services, as well as the Presidential Library and Museum, which attracts Hoover scholars.

CENTRAL IOWA

The side-by-side towns of Clear Lake and Mason City have ties to famous musical figures. Composer Meredith Willson grew up in Mason City. He used his hometown as the model for River City, the setting of his hit Broadway musical, *The Music Man*.

The Legends of Rock and Roll Monument in Clear Lake memorializes Buddy Holly, Richie Valens, and J. D. Richardson, who was better-known as the "Big Bopper." In 1959, after a nearby performance, these rock-and-roll pioneers were killed in a plane crash.

Iowa's capital, cultural center, and largest city is Des Moines. The state capitol rises from a hilltop overlooking the city. Work on this landmark went on for thirteen years until it was finally completed

Herbert Hoover, the thirty-first president of the United States, was born in this modest house in West Branch.

in 1884. In the process, one architect died, one resigned, and the others encountered major challenges in carrying out the ambitious design. The result is a massive building with a central dome covered in gleaming gold leaf and four smaller domes at the corners. Inside is a collection of inaugural gowns worn by the wives of the state's governors.

Iowa has the only state governor's residence open to the public. Terrace Hill is a splendid mansion, built in 1869 for a Des Moines millionaire. In 1976, the estate became the governor's residence. It is open to tourists from March through December.

The small town of Winterset, in Madison County, was the birth-

Des Moines is Iowa's capital and largest city.

place of Marion Michael Morrison, who grew up to be "the Duke"—actor John Wayne. After touring John Wayne's boyhood home, you can make another Hollywood-related excursion. Madison County is the site of half a dozen covered bridges built in the nineteenth century. First made famous by Iowan Robert James Waller's novel *The Bridges of Madison County*, they were then featured in the movie of the same name. All are open to visitors.

WESTERN IOWA

Iowa's northwestern corner contains the state's beautiful "Great Lakes." Scooped out by glaciers, these large, clear lakes are popular resort areas. But they were not always vacation spots. In the 1850s, the Sioux Indians held religious meetings along Spirit Lake and East and West Okoboji Lakes.

In February 1857, a band of Sioux led by the rebel leader Inkpaduta discovered that a handful of white settlers had staked claims and built cabins along the Indians' sacred shores. This discovery, coupled with the unusual harshness of the winter, sparked a tragedy.

Moving swiftly from one isolated house to another, Inkpaduta

Picturesque Roseman Bridge is one of six nineteenth-century covered bridges in Madison County. Made famous by a best-selling novel, the bridges have become popular tourist destinations.

and his followers killed thirty-four of the settlers and carried off several captives. The Spirit Lake Massacre, as the incident was called, was perhaps the saddest chapter in the history of white-Indian relationships in Iowa.

Although a search party set out, it never caught Inkpaduta. Eventually, two of the prisoners were freed by their captors. Abbie Gardner, whose family perished in the attack, wrote extensively about her experience. The Gardner cabin still stands in Arnolds Park, overlooking West Okoboji Lake.

Sioux City, on Iowa's Nebraska border, rose to prominence as a meatpacking center, but students of architecture know it as the site of the Woodbury County Courthouse. Built in 1918 by architects who had studied with the master Louis Sullivan, the courthouse features leaded stained-glass windows and ornamental sculptures in terra cotta. In designing the building, the architects incorporated some of the principles of the prairie style, a kind of architecture intended to harmonize with the rolling Midwestern prairies.

A different sort of judicial architecture can be found in Council Bluffs. Prisoners kept in the "Squirrel Cage Jail," built in 1885, had no chance of escape. Their cells lacked doors!

The jail is a circular, three-tier structure containing wedge-shaped cells; ten of these make up each metal drum. To reach one of his charges, the jailer turned a crank until the prisoner's cell aligned with the jail's only door. The Squirrel Cage was used until 1969.

Iowa has more wonders than can be described in a short book. Hugh Sidey, contributing editor of *Time* magazine, put it well when he said that his native state possesses "a subtle magic."

These colorful balloons lend an exotic air to a serene landscape near Indianola.

IOWA

THE FLAG: *The state flag has three panels, one for each of the state's colors. In the middle panel, against a white background, is a reproduction of the eagle from the state seal carrying a streamer with the state motto.*

THE SEAL: *In the foreground a soldier holds an American flag with 13 stars for the original 13 states in his right hand and a gun in his left hand. A plow, a sheaf of wheat, and a sickle represent agriculture. To the soldier's right are a pile of pig lead and a lead furnace. The Mississippi River and the steamboat in the background are symbolic of commerce. The state seal was adopted in 1847.*

STATE SURVEY

Statehood: December 28, 1846

Origin of Name: Named for the Iowa Indian tribe who inhabited this area. The word Iowa has been interpreted to mean "beautiful land."

Nickname: Hawkeye State

Capital: Des Moines

Motto: Our Liberties We Prize, and Our Rights We Will Maintain

Bird: Eastern goldfinch

Flower: Wild rose

Tree: Oak

Stone: Geode

Eastern goldfinch

Wild rose

THE SONG OF IOWA

Iowa has no official state song, but "The Song of Iowa" has been accepted and sung as such since its composition by S. H. M. Byers in 1897. Its composer gave the following account of the inspiration for the song:

> At the great battle of Lookout Mountain [in Tennessee in 1863 during the Civil War] I was captured . . . and taken to Libby Prison, Richmond, Va. I was there seven months in one room. The rebel bands often passed the prison, and for our discomfiture, sometimes played the tune "Maryland, My Maryland," set to Southern and bitter words. Hearing it once through our barred windows, I said to myself, "I would like some day to put that tune to loyal words."

Words by S. H. M. Byers

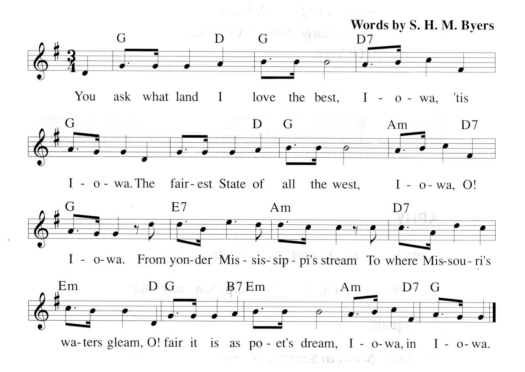

And she has maids whose laughing eyes,
Iowa, O! Iowa,
To him who loves were Paradise,
Iowa, O! Iowa.
O! happiest fate that e'er was known,
Such eyes to shine for one alone.
To call such beauty all his own.
Iowa, O! Iowa.

See yonder fields of tasselled corn,
Iowa, in Iowa,
Where Plenty fills her golden horn,
Iowa, in Iowa.
See how her wondrous prairies shine
To yonder sunset's purpling line.
O! happy land, O! land of mine,
Iowa, O! Iowa.

Go read the story of thy past,
Iowa, O! Iowa.
What glorious deeds, what fame thou hast!
Iowa, O! Iowa.
So long as time's great cycle runs,
Or nations weep their fallen sons,
Thou'lt not forget thy patriot sons,
Iowa, O! Iowa.

GEOGRAPHY

Highest Point: 1,670 feet, in northern Osceola County

Lowest Point: 480 feet, along the Mississippi River at Keokuk

Area: 56,275 square miles

Greatest Distance, North to South: 214 miles

Greatest Distance, East to West: 332 miles

Bordering States: Minnesota to the north, Wisconsin and Illinois to the east, Missouri to the south, and Nebraska and South Dakota to the west

Hottest Recorded Temperature: 118°F at Keokuk on July 20, 1934

Coldest Recorded Temperature: -47°F at Washta on January 12, 1912

Average Annual Precipitation: 32 inches

Major Rivers: Boyer, Cedar, Chariton, Des Moines, Floyd, Iowa, Little Sioux, Maquoketa, Mississippi, Missouri, Nodaway, Skunk, Thompson

Major Lakes: Clear, East Okoboji, Spirit, Storm, West Okoboji

Trees: ash, balsam, basswood, cedar, cottonwood, elm, maple, oak, walnut, willow

Wild Plants: aster, avens, bloodroot, Canadian thistle, dog fennel, golden-rod, honeysuckle, mayapple, mesquite, milkweed, prairie aster, prairie lily, rose, shooting star

Animals: beaver, chipmunk, coyote, deer, fox, gopher, mink, muskrat, opossum, rabbit, raccoon, rattlesnake, squirrel, skunk

Birds: blue jay, Canada goose, cardinal, duck, hawk, partridge, prairie chicken, red-winged blackbird, robin, starling, tufted titmouse

Fish: bass, bluegill, carp, catfish, crappie, northern pike, perch, sucker, walleye

Wood duck

Endangered Animals: bald eagle, Indiana bat, Iowa snail, peregrine falcon, pearly mussel, piping plover, sturgeon

Endangered Plants: eastern prairie fringed orchid, Mead's milkweed, northern wild monkshood, prairie bush clover, western prairie fringed orchid

western prairie fringed orchid

TIMELINE

Iowa History

c. 500 B.C. Mound builders inhabit area

1600s Siouan ethnic groups, including Iowa, Omaha, Oto, Missouri, and Sioux (or Dakota) arrive in present-day Iowa

1673 French explorers Father Jacques Marquette and Louis Jolliet become the first Europeans to see present-day Iowa

1733 Sauk and Mesquakie Indians arrive in Iowa after being forced out of Wisconsin by the French

1788 Julien Dubuque, Iowa's first white settler, begins mining land near present-day Dubuque

1803 United States acquires Iowa from France in the Louisiana Purchase

1808 The U.S. Army builds Fort Madison, the first U.S. military outpost in Iowa

1820 Congress passes the Missouri Compromise, making Iowa a free (non-slave) territory

1830 Dr. Isaac Galland establishes the first school in Iowa

1832 The U.S. Army defeats Sauk and Mesquakie Indians led by Chief Black Hawk in the Black Hawk War

1836 Congress creates the Territory of Wisconsin, which includes Iowa, Minnesota, and most of the Dakotas

1838 The Territory of Iowa is created

1846 Iowa becomes the 29th state

1853 Iowa's first public library opens at Fairfield

1857 The state legislature adopts Iowa's present constitution; the state capital moves to Des Moines

1867 The first railroad across Iowa is completed

1868 An amendment to the state constitution gives black males the right to vote

1869 Iowan Annabella Bobb Mansfield becomes first woman admitted to the practice of law in the United States

1890 Iowa becomes the nation's leading producer of corn

1913 Engineers complete the Keokuk Dam

1917 Iowa begins an extensive road-building program

1928 Iowan Herbert Hoover is elected president of the United States

1930 Iowan Susan Glaspell wins the Pulitzer Prize in drama for *Alison's House*

1953 State legislature creates nine-member state board of education

1985 State lottery is established to raise revenue

1989 Plane crash in Sioux City kills 111 people

1991 Legalized riverboat gambling begins

1993 Heavy rains result in major floods, causing more than $2 billion worth of damage

ECONOMY

Agricultural Products: beef, cattle, corn, dairy products, hogs, soybeans, wheat

Manufactured Products: appliances, chemicals, electrical equipment, fabricated metal products, farm machinery, food products, furniture

Natural Resources: clay, coal, gravel, limestone, sand, shale

Hereford cows and calves

Business and Trade: communication, finance, insurance, real estate, retail trade, transportation, wholesale trade

CALENDAR OF CELEBRATIONS

Sac City Kiwanis Kite Tournament Kite-flying enthusiasts enjoy the country's oldest kiting tournament here every April. The Iowan sky is speckled with thousands of kites, ranging from homemade paper kites to high-tech dual-control featherweight stunt kites.

Waterfest Weekend Visitors take to the water for two days of summer fun during this festival on the Sioux City and South Sioux City banks of the Missouri River every June. Sports tournaments and water-ski shows are mixed with the carefree atmosphere of a carnival.

Sturgis Falls Celebration/Cedar Basin Jazz Festival Tap your toes to more than 20 Dixieland bands that liven up this annual street fair held during the last weekend in June.

Fourth of July Weekend Fireworks aren't the only thing that bring a bang to Sioux City on July 4. Music lovers get a special treat with a blues music fest. Local and national talent such as Santana, Dr. John, and the Neville Brothers provide the entertainment.

College Hill Arts Festival Mid-July brings fabulous art to the University of Northern Iowa campus in Cedar Falls. Over 75 Midwestern artists show their original works and offer demonstrations in various media.

RAGBRAI (The Register's Annual Great Bicycle Race Across Iowa) The longest, largest, and oldest touring bicycle ride in the world, RAGBRAI celebrates Iowa's beautiful countryside during the last week of July. It attracts cyclists from all 50 states and 14 foreign countries. The route is never exactly the same, so many Iowa towns have the chance to open their homes to participants to make this a real statewide celebration.

Nordic Fest Decorah honors its Norwegian ancestors during the annual festival held the last weekend in July. Visitors can sample the food, dancing, and music for an authentic taste of Scandinavia. They can also explore exhibits on woodworking, Norwegian knife-making, rosemaling, and weaving. Children can enjoy the storytellers, rock throws, puppet shows, and the Kilties Drum & Bugle Corps.

Nordic Fest

Tanager Place Summerfest Colorful hot-air balloons dot the Iowa sky during the first weekend in August. The Amana Colonies host this festival that also features a radio-controlled airplane rally and nonstop live music.

Gus Macker Basketball Tournament Thousands of basketball fans converge on Cedar Falls in early August to participate in this nationally known basketball tournament. Players of all ages enjoy competing at this 3-on-3 tournament.

Cedar Trail Festival Thousands come to Cedar Park in August to take special advantage of its 30 miles of beautiful recreational trails. Bring your dog for the dog walk, take a spin during the nighttime bike ride, and enjoy live music concerts along the way.

Holzfest Families enjoy the Midwest's greatest wood show every August in the Amana Colonies. In addition to seeing woodworking displays, visitors can dance, listen to music, and enjoy the homemade food.

Old Time Power Show August is the time to revisit the pioneer settlement days in Cedar Falls. The city marks the end of summer with tractor pulls, parades, flea markets, and a display of antique farm equipment.

Eulenspiegel Puppet Theatre The only professional puppet troupe in Iowa brings folk and fairy tales to life at the Riverside Theatre in Iowa City. Performances are offered three times a year between October and June.

STATE STARS

Adrian Constantine (Cap) Anson (1851–1922) was known as the greatest baseball player of the 19th century. Born in Marshalltown, he led the Chicago White Stockings to five pennants and became the first major-league player to get 3,000 hits.

Leon Bismarck (Bix) Beiderbecke (1903–1931) was an accomplished jazz musician who won acclaim during his short life. Born in Davenport, he won audiences' hearts with his cornet solos. During his career, he performed with many great jazz bands, but his peers regarded his small jazz combos as his greatest success. Beiderbecke composed "Singin' the Blues" and "In a Mist."

Black Hawk (1767–1838) was a Sauk Indian chief who fought on the side of the British during the War of 1812. He believed his people had been tricked into ceding their lands east of the Mississippi River to the U.S. government and refused to move west of the Mississippi. He fought the Black Hawk War in 1832 to defend Indian lands but was defeated.

Amelia Jenks Bloomer (1818–1894) advocated Prohibition and women's rights. As an adult, she settled in Council Bluffs, where she headed

Adrian Anson

the Iowa Woman Suffrage Association. She popularized loose-fitting pants for women that came to be called "bloomers."

Norman Ernest Borlaug (1914–   ), who was born in Cresco, developed new varieties of wheat during his career as an agricultural scientist. In the 1950s and 1960s, the wheat developed by Borlaug was introduced into India, Pakistan, and Mexico. He won the 1970 Nobel Peace Prize for his food production work.

Amelia Jenks Bloomer

Johnny Carson

Johnny Carson (1925–   ) is a popular entertainer who hosted *The Tonight Show* for 30 years. His success as a talk show host has been attributed to his easygoing manner and ability to get people to talk about themselves. He was born in Corning.

Carrie Chapman Catt (1859–1947) helped form the Iowa Woman Suffrage Association. An educator as well as social reformer, she served as principal and superintendent of Mason City schools. She led the campaign that resulted in the ratification of the 19th Amendment to the Constitution in 1920, which gave women the right to vote.

Carrie Chapman Catt

Lee De Forest (1873–1961), an inventor born in Council Bluffs, was known as the "Father of Radio" because he created transmitting and receiving devices. He equipped U.S. Navy ships with wireless telephones and inaugurated radio news broadcasts.

George Gallup

Lee De Forest

George Gallup (1901–1984) was a public-opinion expert. Born in Jefferson, he founded the American Institute of Public Opinion, which created the famous Gallup Poll.

Hamlin Garland (1860–1940) grew up facing the hardships of pioneer life on the Iowa frontier and turned his experiences into widely read books. He wrote *Main-Travelled Roads* and *A Son of the Middle Border*, which was his autobiography. In 1921, he won the Pulitzer Prize in biography for *A Daughter of the Middle Border*.

Susan Glaspell (1882–1948) was born in Davenport. She and her husband founded the prestigious Provincetown Playhouse. A novelist and playwright, she won the 1930 Pulitzer Prize in drama for *Alison's House*.

Fred Grandy (1948–   ), who was born in Sioux City, played Gopher on the television series *The Love Boat*. He entered politics in the mid-1980s and won his first term to the U.S. House of Representatives in 1987.

Herbert Clark Hoover (1874–1964) was president of the United States from 1929 to 1933. He earned a fortune as a geologist and mining engineer and then entered public service. Hoover served as head of the American Relief Commission in London and the Commission for Relief in Belgium during World War I. Prior to being elected president, this West Branch native served as secretary of commerce under President Calvin Coolidge.

Glenn Miller (1904–1944) was a bandleader who headed one of the most famous big bands. Born in Clarinda, he composed many famous songs, including "In the Mood," "Tuxedo Junction," "Little Brown Jug," and "Moonlight Serenade."

Glenn Miller and his orchestra

Alfred (1861–1919), **Charles** (1863–1926), and **John** (1866–1936) **Ringling**, who organized and founded the Ringling Brothers Circus, were

The Ringling family, with Alfred and Charles (standing second and fifth from left) and John (sitting at left)

born in MacGregor. They combined their circus with the Barnum and Bailey Circus to form the "Greatest Show on Earth."

James Alfred Van Allen (1914–   ), who was born in Mount Pleasant, headed the department of physics and astronomy at the University of Iowa for more than 30 years. His cosmic ray detection device discovered the two radiation belts around the earth that are now called the Van Allen belts.

Henry Agard Wallace (1888–1965) was born in Adair County and gained prominence for helping farmers by popularizing the hardier and more productive hybrid corn seed. He served as secretary of agriculture and vice president under President Franklin Roosevelt. He was one of the most important figures of the New Deal period, promoting such controversial programs as paying farmers not to grow crops.

John Wayne (1907–1979) was born in Winterset. He made over 200 films during his acting career. Wayne usually portrayed strong heroes in his action

John Wayne

movies, which include *Stagecoach, Red River,* and *Sands of Iwo Jima.* He won an Academy Award for best actor in 1969 for his role in *True Grit.*

Meredith Willson (1902–1984) wrote the famous Broadway musical *The Music Man.* Willson used his hometown of Mason City as a basis for the fictional River City, Iowa, in the musical.

Garfield Arthur Wood (left)
in Miss America IX

Garfield Arthur Wood (1880–1971) devised the PT boat used in World War II. This sportsman and industrialist from Mapleton also set world records in speedboat and hydroplane racing.

Grant Wood (1892–1942) portrayed the Midwest in his realistic paintings. His best-known work, *American Gothic,* features a Midwestern farmer and his daughter. He was born in Anamosa.

TOUR THE STATE

Amana Colonies Seven quaint villages rest in the lush Iowa River valley 20 miles southwest of Cedar Rapids. Once run by a religious society, the area is now a 26,000-acre National Historic Landmark. The heritage of the German settlers remains, as residents still produce high-quality products, including food, furniture, and appliances. Visitors can watch the craftworkers build furniture and weave fabrics.

Boone and Scenic Valley Railroad Enjoy a taste of the transportation of yesteryear. This railroad takes travelers through Iowa's scenic countryside and over one of the highest bridges in the United States.

Danish Windmill See an authentic windmill from Denmark. Built in 1848, the windmill was dismantled, shipped to Iowa, and then rebuilt on its present site at Elk Horn.

DeSoto National Wildlife Refuge Visitors come here in the spring and fall to see thousands of duck and geese as they migrate through the Missouri River valley. The visitors' center features wildlife exhibits and artifacts from a sunken steamboat.

Effigy Mounds National Monument At this site, you can see the artifacts from Iowa's prehistoric Indian population. These mounds near McGregor are in the shapes of birds, snakes, bears, and wolves.

Herbert Hoover's Birthplace The white cottage in West Branch where Herbert Hoover was born is surrounded by a beautiful park. A restored blacksmith shop and a library of Hoover's public papers are also there. Hoover was buried at the site in 1964.

Living History Farms Visitors can walk from the present to the past and back on these farms in Des Moines. This

Pioneer Days, Living History Farms

large open-air museum depicts Iowa farm life from pioneer days to the present. Costumed guides demonstrate skills and crafts on period farms.

Paddle-wheel Riverboats You can enjoy fine dining and family entertainment while cruising on a Mississippi riverboat. Visitors take an interesting passage through the Mississippi's lock and dam system.

Vesterheim Norwegian-American Museum As you walk through these 15 historic buildings that cover nearly a city block, you are seeing the most comprehensive collection of artifacts devoted to a single immigrant ethnic group in America. Norwegian-Americans began collecting objects in the 1870s so they could preserve their history. Over 21,000 objects are housed at this site in Decorah, including a horse-head bowl dating from 1816 and an authentic interior of a log house built in 1850.

Iowa Firefighters Memorial This bronze statue of a firefighter rescuing a child honors the sacrifices made by Iowan firefighters. Located in Coralville, the sculpture stands before a granite wall that bears the names of the professional and volunteer firefighters for whom the sculpture was created.

Museum of Natural History Learn more about the natural world and its inhabitants in the oldest museum of natural history west of the Mississippi. The Iowa City museum features fascinating dioramas, including orangutans in a Borneo jungle and a walrus collected by Arctic explorer Robert Peary. The Iowa Hall Gallery features a life-sized giant ground sloth among its many Iowa geologic fossils.

Devonian Fossil Gorge The massive floods of 1993 eroded a 15-foot-deep channel exposing the underlying Devonian-age seafloor. Visitors can see ancient fossils and exposed rocks from Iowa's geologic past.

The University of Iowa Museum of Art The centerpiece of this museum is one of the nation's most important collections of African sculpture. Changing international exhibits and selections from among the museum's 8,500 works of art delight visitors year-round.

Laura Ingalls Wilder Park and Museum The childhood home of this popular writer is found 12 miles north of Decorah. The house is furnished with period pieces that give visitors a look at the circumstances of Wilder's early years.

The Locust School This historic schoolhouse in Decorah was built in 1854 and operated for 106 years.

Tiny Tim's Colony Christmas Enjoy German and American food at the popular Ronneberg Restaurant and then view its stunning collection of beautiful Christmas items from around the world.

Black Hawk Park There's plenty to do at this 1,276-acre park in Cedar Falls. You can play softball and baseball, enjoy hiking trails, practice your aim on the rifle and archery range, or visit the wildlife refuge.

Loess Hills In western Iowa along the bluffs that border the Missouri Valley is a dramatic natural landmark that spans nearly 10,000 acres. Loess is a common geologic material found in the Midwest. Here the loess reaches 100 feet thick and is the dominant element of the terrain.

FUN FACTS

The Pottawattamie County Jail in Council Bluffs was called the "lazy Susan jail." Pie-shaped jail cells rotated around a central core. Once a prisoner entered a cell from the core, the cell was rotated to seal it off. In use from 1885 to 1969, the jail has been restored and is now open to the public.

Dubuque is home to the shortest, steepest operating railroad in the United States. The track is 296 feet long and rises at a 60-degree incline to a height of 189 feet.

The Red Delicious apple was developed near East Peru. Originally called the Hawkeye apple when Jesse Hiatt entered it in an apple contest, it was renamed when the Stark Brothers Nursery purchased the rights to the fruit.

FIND OUT MORE

If you'd like to find out more about Iowa, check your local library or bookstore for these titles:

GENERAL STATE BOOKS

Aylesworth, Thomas. *Western Great Lakes: Illinois, Iowa, Minnesota, Wisconsin.* New York: Chelsea House, 1996.

Kent, Deborah. *America the Beautiful: Iowa.* Chicago: Children's Press, 1991.

LaDoux, Rita C. *Iowa.* Minneapolis: Lerner Publications, 1992.

Thompson, Kathleen. *Iowa.* Milwaukee: Raintree, 1986.

BOOKS OF SPECIAL INTEREST

Biographies of Notable Iowans

Clinton, Susan. *Herbert Hoover: Thirty-first President of the United States.* Chicago: Children's Press, 1988.

Duggleby, John. *Artist in Overalls: The Life of Grant Wood.* San Francisco: Chronicle Books, 1996.

San Souci, Robert D., and Max Ginsberg, illus. *Kate Shelley: Bound for Legend.* New York: Dial Books for Young Readers, 1994.

Fiction

Ambrus, Victor. *Stranger in the Storm.* London/New York: Abelard-Schuman, 1972.

Edwards, Michelle. *Eve and Smithy: An Iowa Tale.* New York: Lothrop, Lee & Shepard Books, 1994.

Hall, Lynn. *Too Near the Sun.* Chicago: Follett, 1970.

_____ and Allen Davis, illus. *Ghost of the Great River Inn.* Chicago: Follett, 1981.

Horvath, Polly. *No More Cornflakes.* New York: Farrar, Strauss, and Giroux, 1990.

Irwin, Hadley. *We Are Mesquakie, We Are One.* Old Westbury, New York: Feminist Press, 1980.

Naylor, Phyllis Reynolds. *Maudie in the Middle.* New York: Atheneum, 1988.

Olsen, Violet. *The Growing Season.* New York: Atheneum, 1982.

Thomas, Jane R. *The Princess in the Pigpen.* New York: Clarion Books, 1989.

Walker, Mary Alexander. *Brad's Box.* New York: Atheneum, 1988.

VIDEOS

Portrait of America: Iowa. New York: Ambrose Video Pub., 1983.

MUSIC

Beiderbecke, Bix. *Bix Lives!* Compact disc recording of selections by Bix and his orchestra. Bluebird, 1989.

Willson, Meredith. *The Music Man.* Compact disc recording of score from musical. Capitol Records, SW-990.

INTERNET

Go to www.state.ia.us to find Iowa's home page. It provides information on government, business, education, and tourism and also contains links to many sites with details on all aspects of the Hawkeye State.

INDEX

Page numbers for illustrations are in boldface.